1

How To Draw Chibis Like A Manga Artist

Advice from the Experts: How To Draw Chibis

Chibis

By: Gala Publication

Published By:

Gala Publication
ISBN-13: **978-1522708155**
ISBN-10: **1522708154**

©Copyright 2015 – Gala Publication

Index

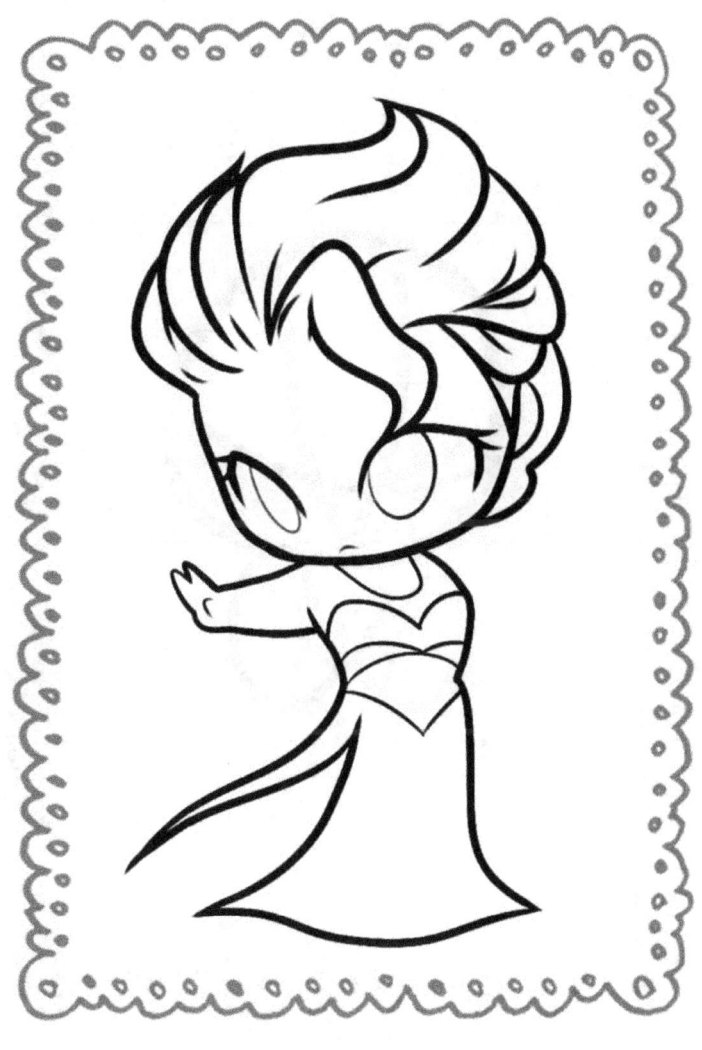

ELSA

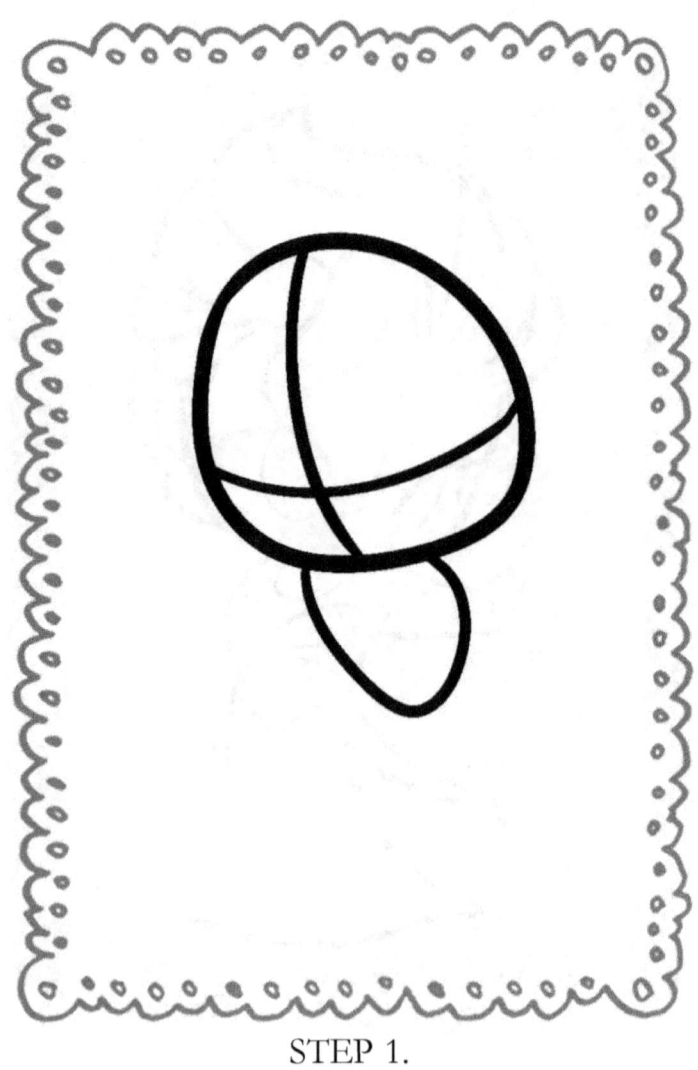

STEP 1.

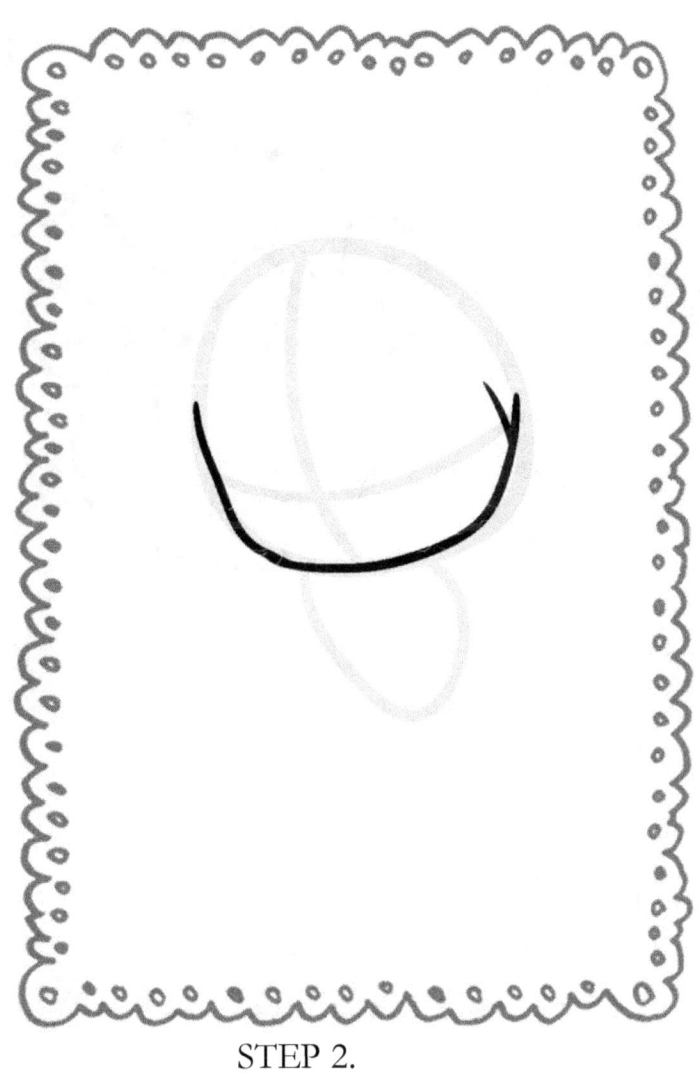

STEP 2.

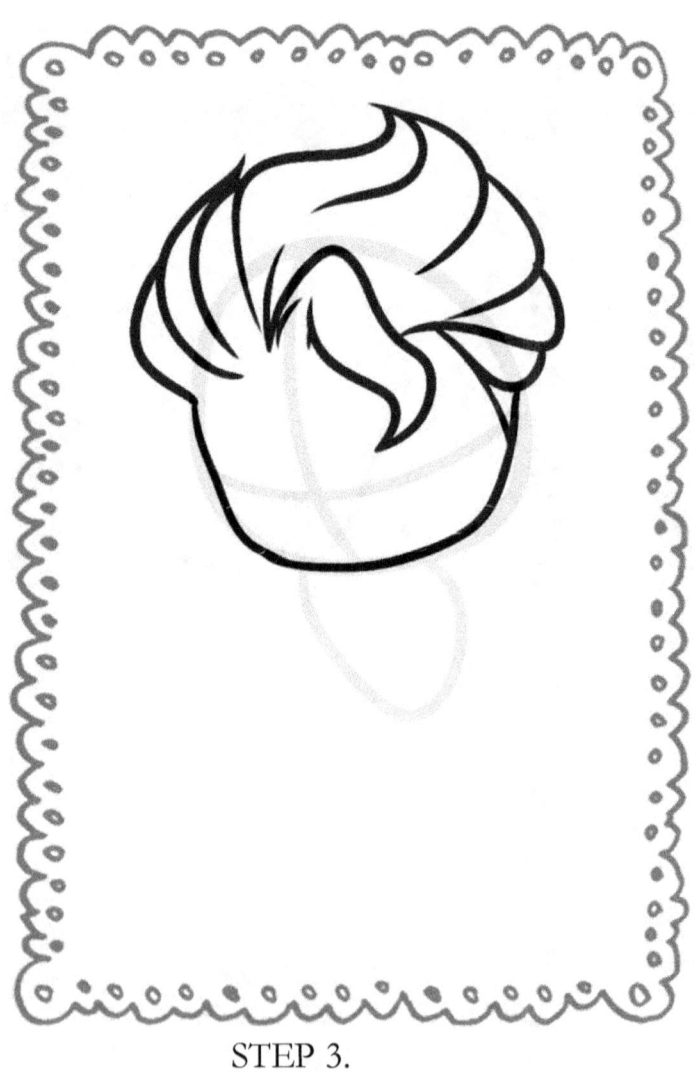

STEP 3.

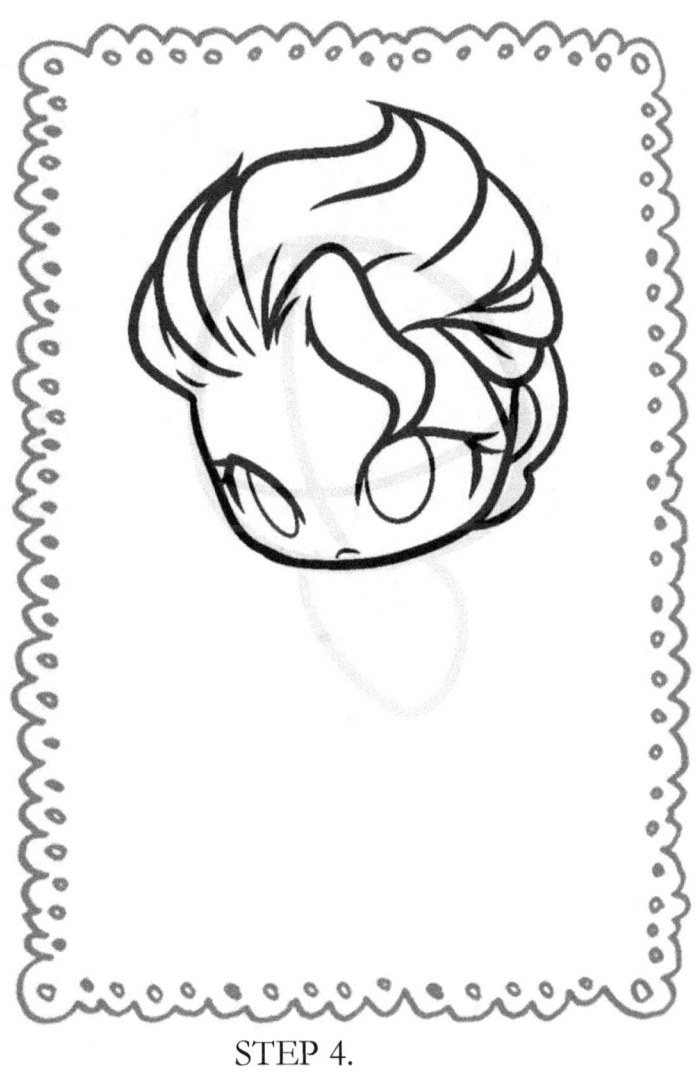

STEP 4.

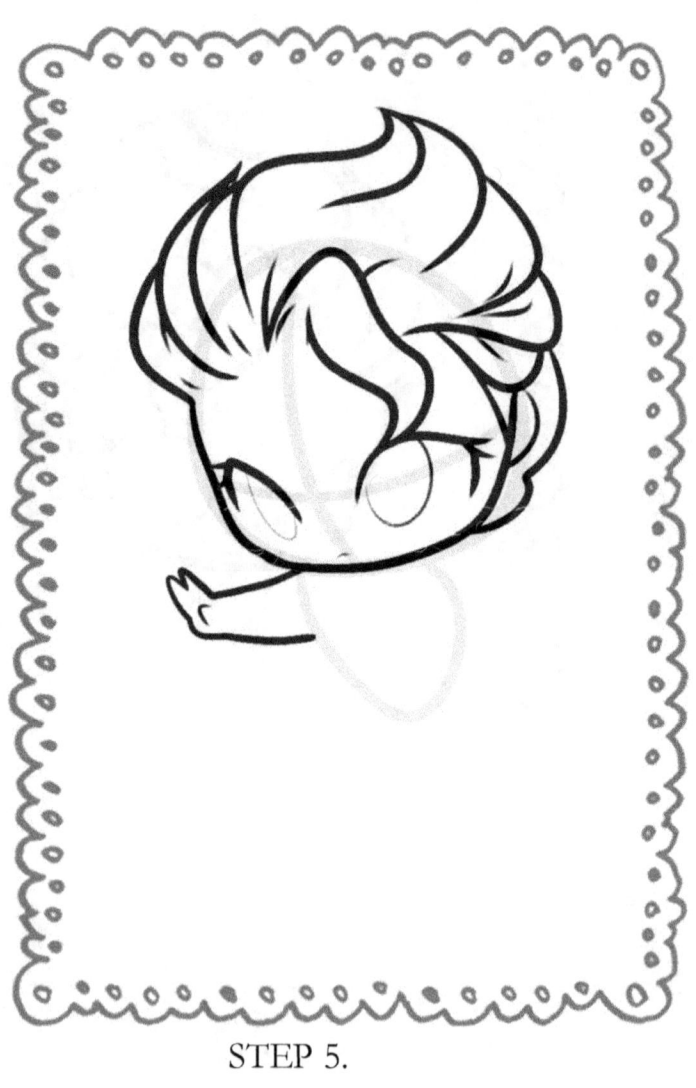

STEP 5.

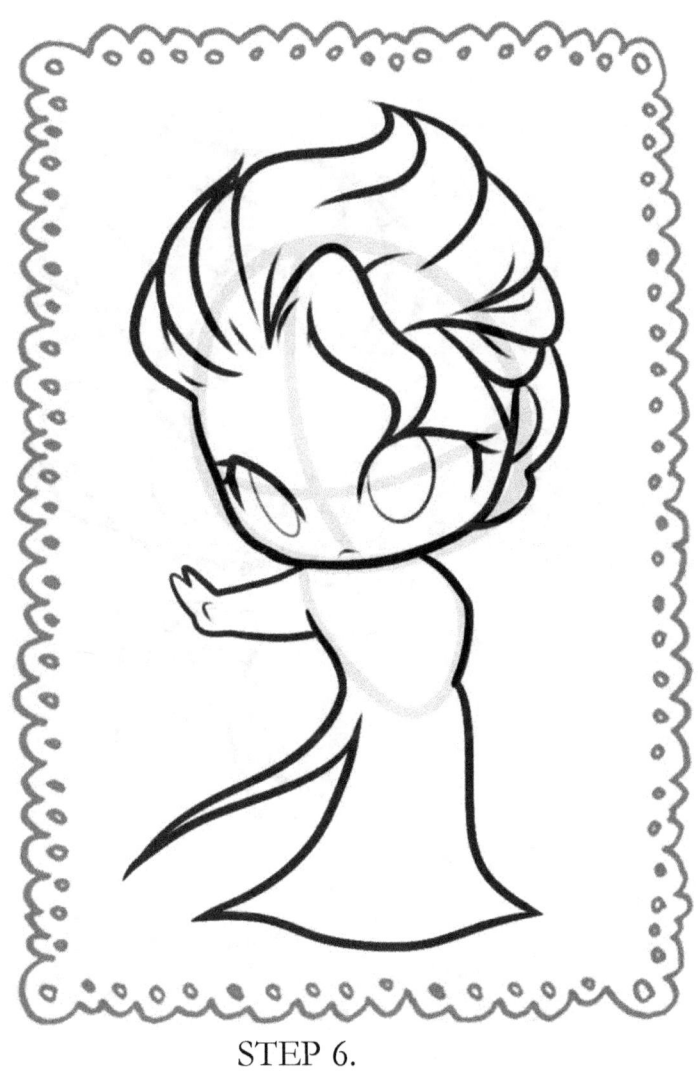

STEP 6.

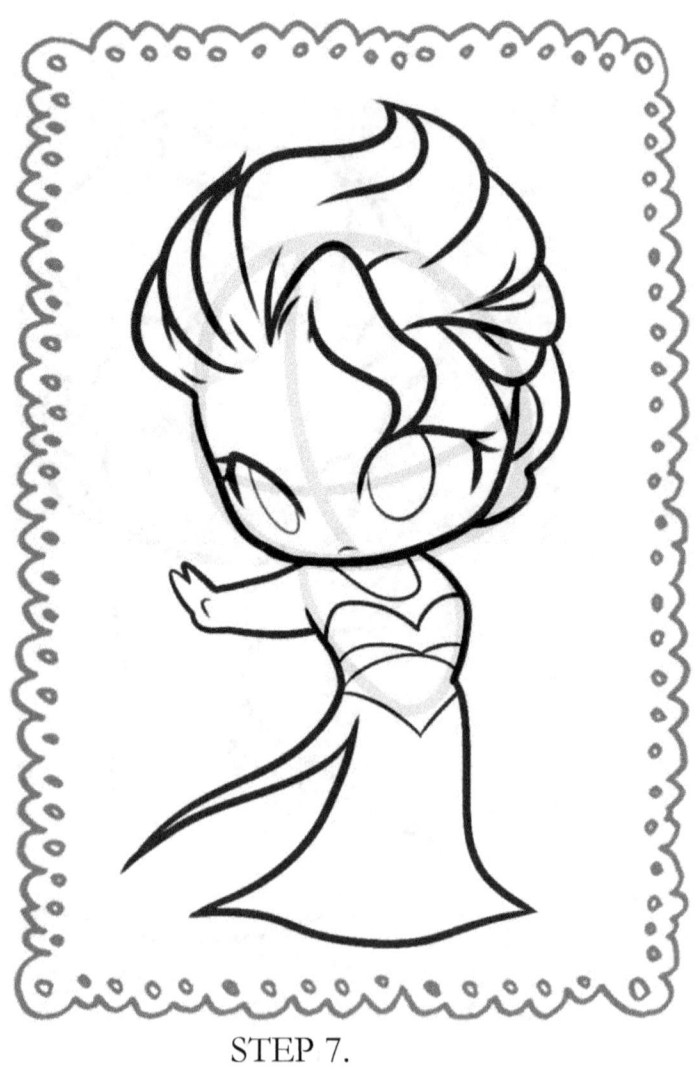

STEP 7.

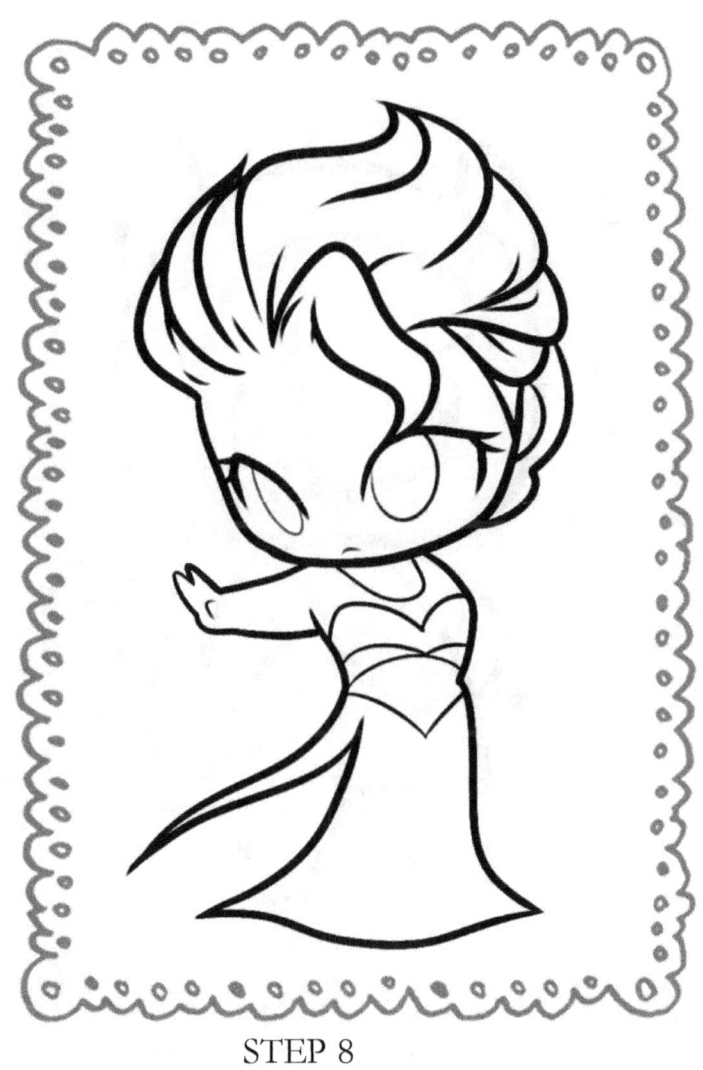

STEP 8

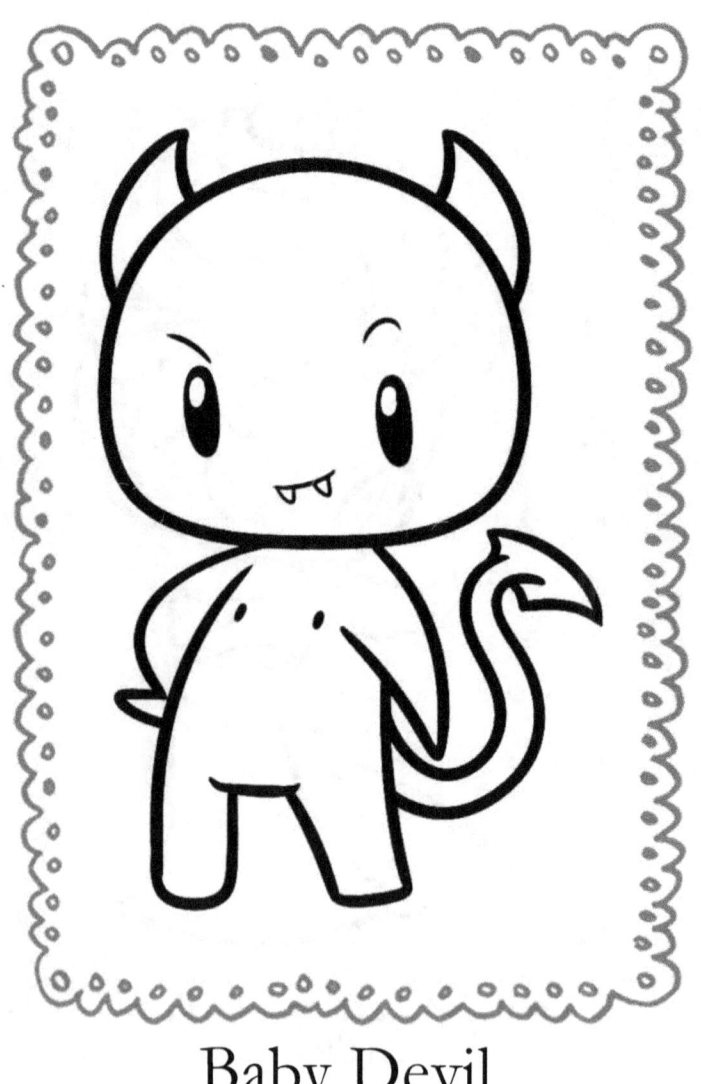

Baby Devil

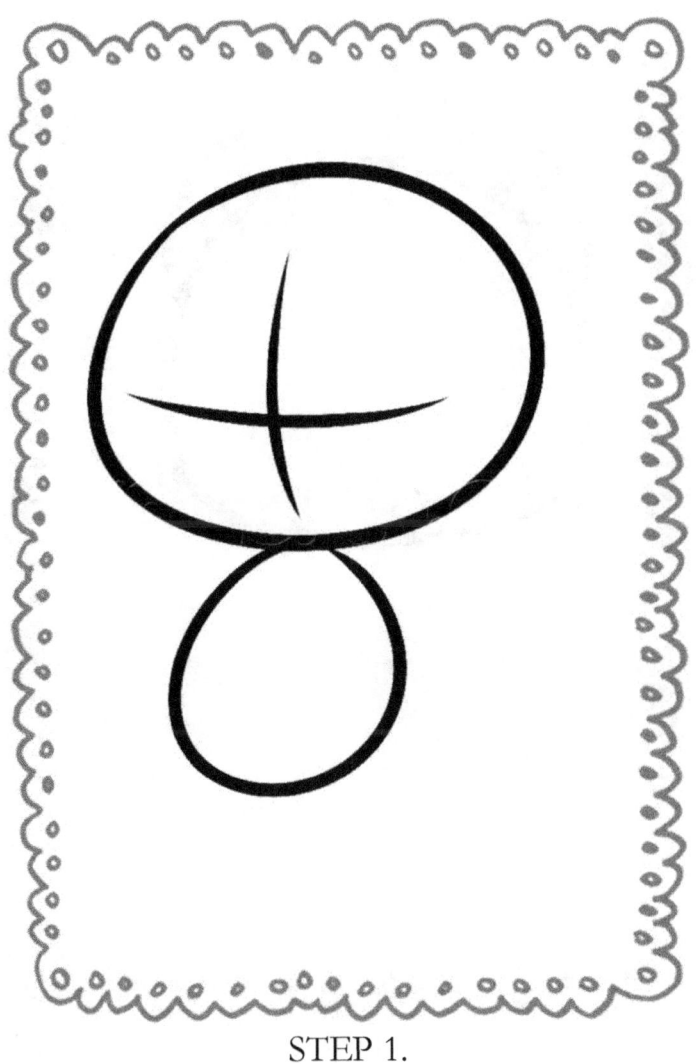

STEP 1.

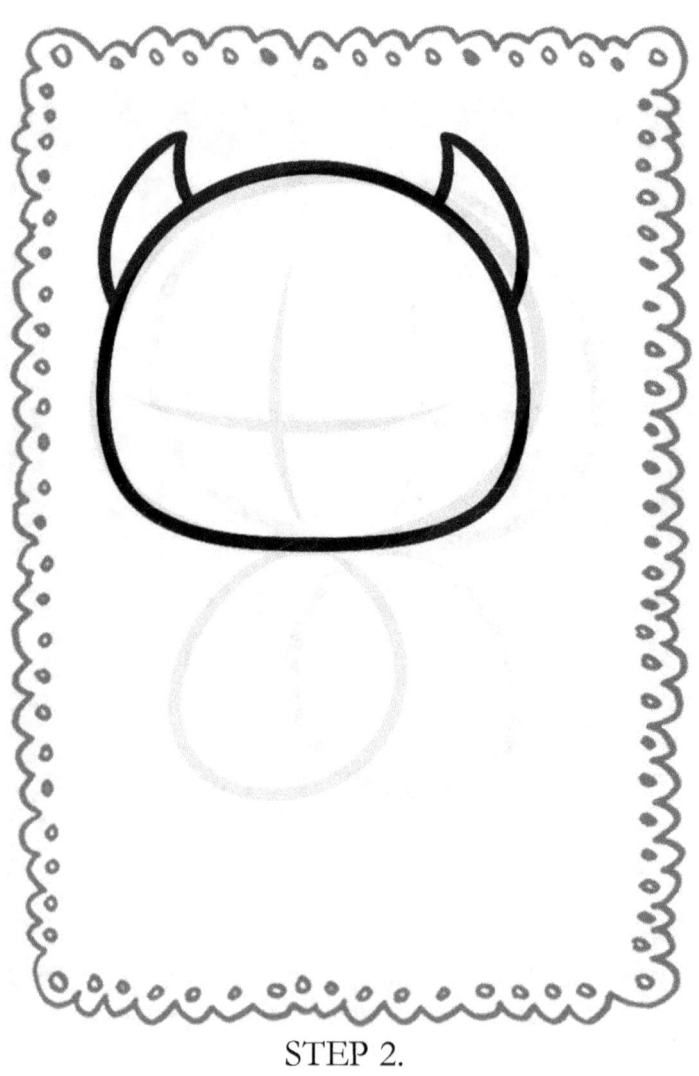

STEP 2.

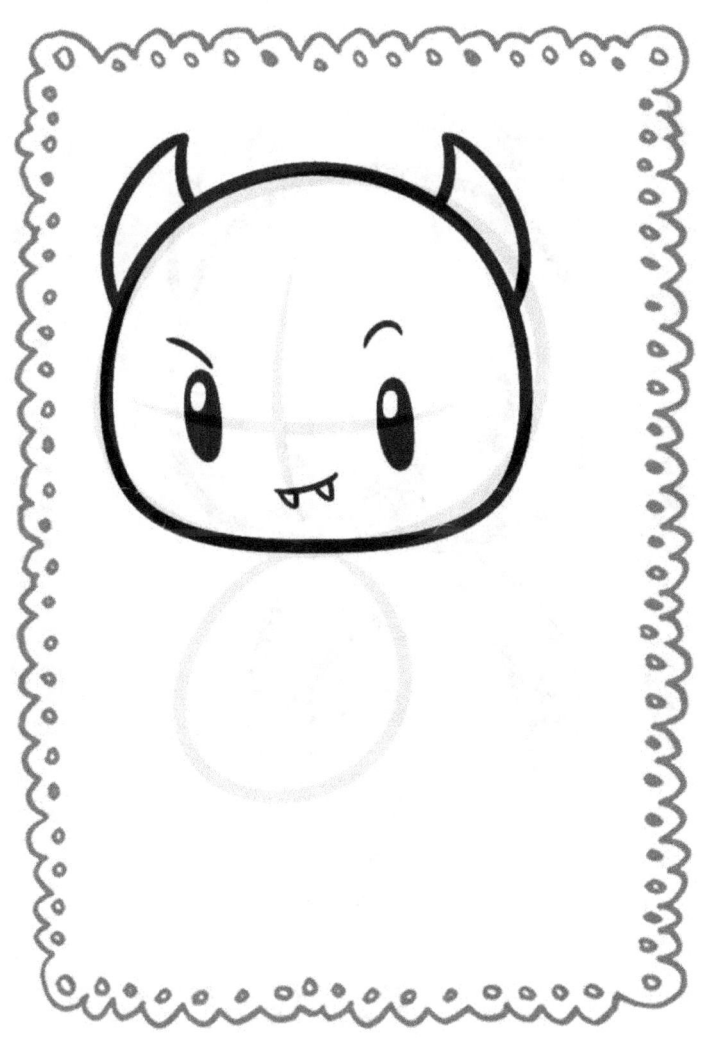

STEP 3.

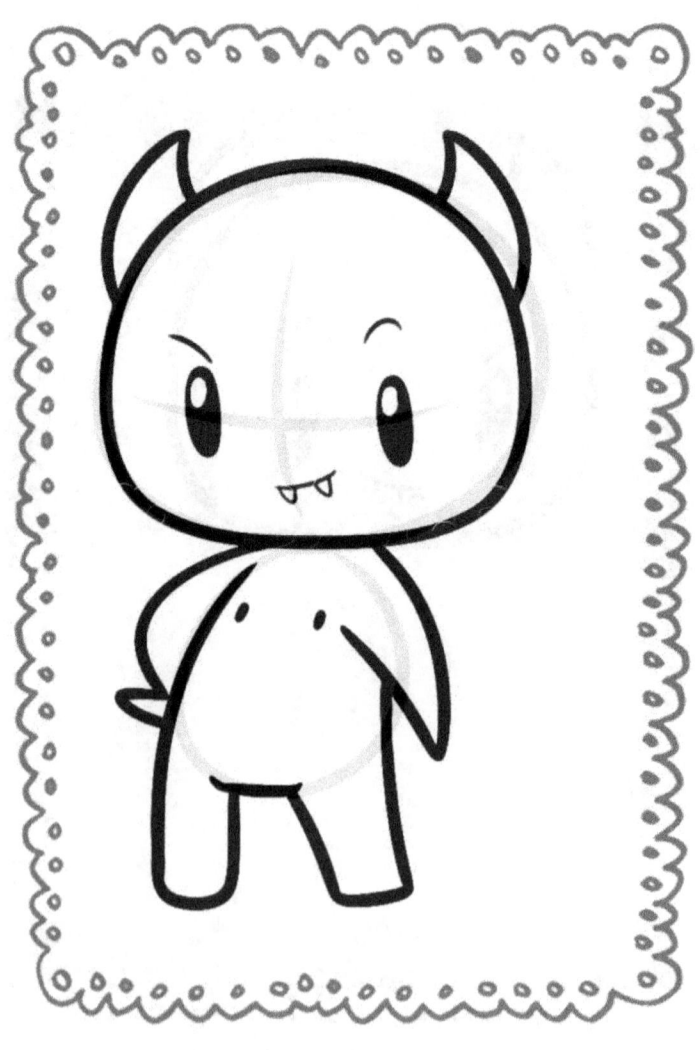

STEP 4.

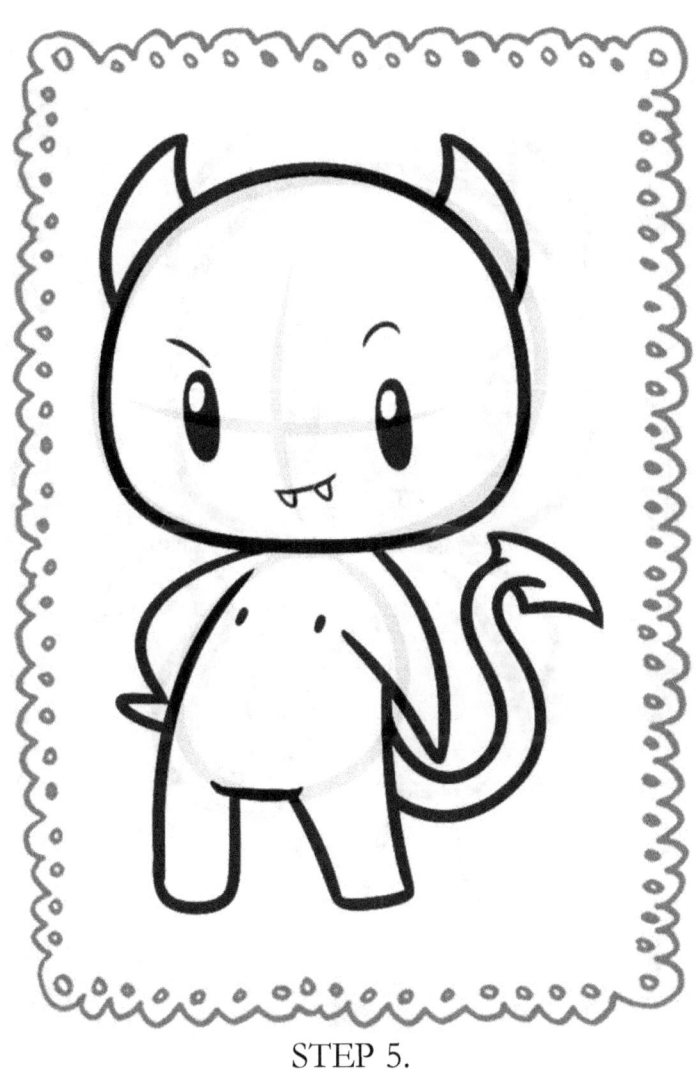

STEP 5.

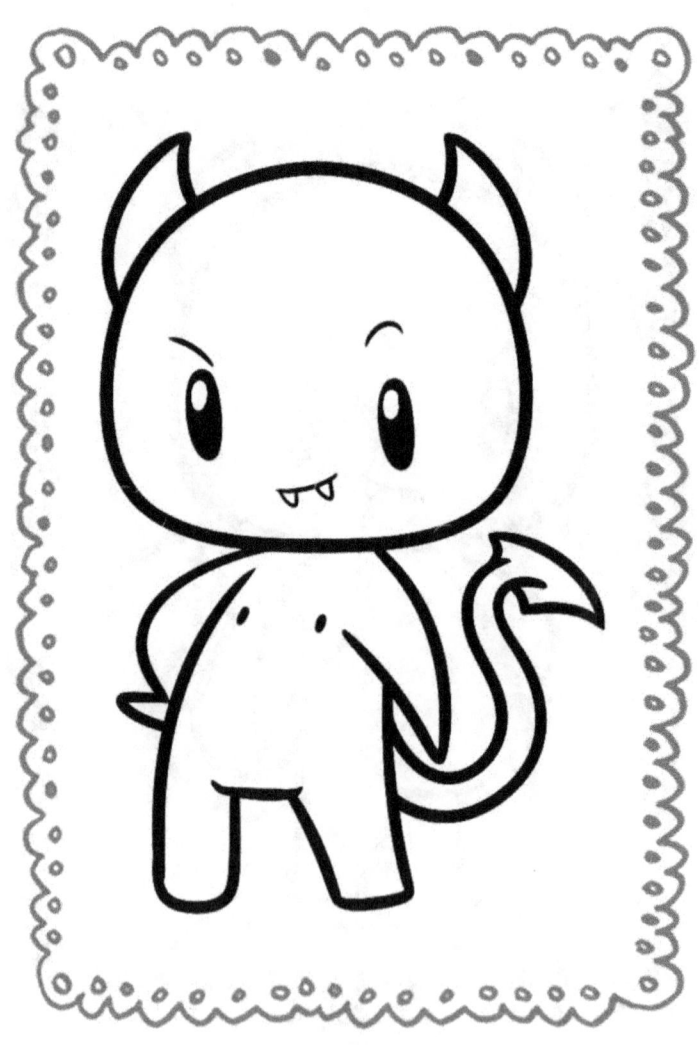

STEP 6.

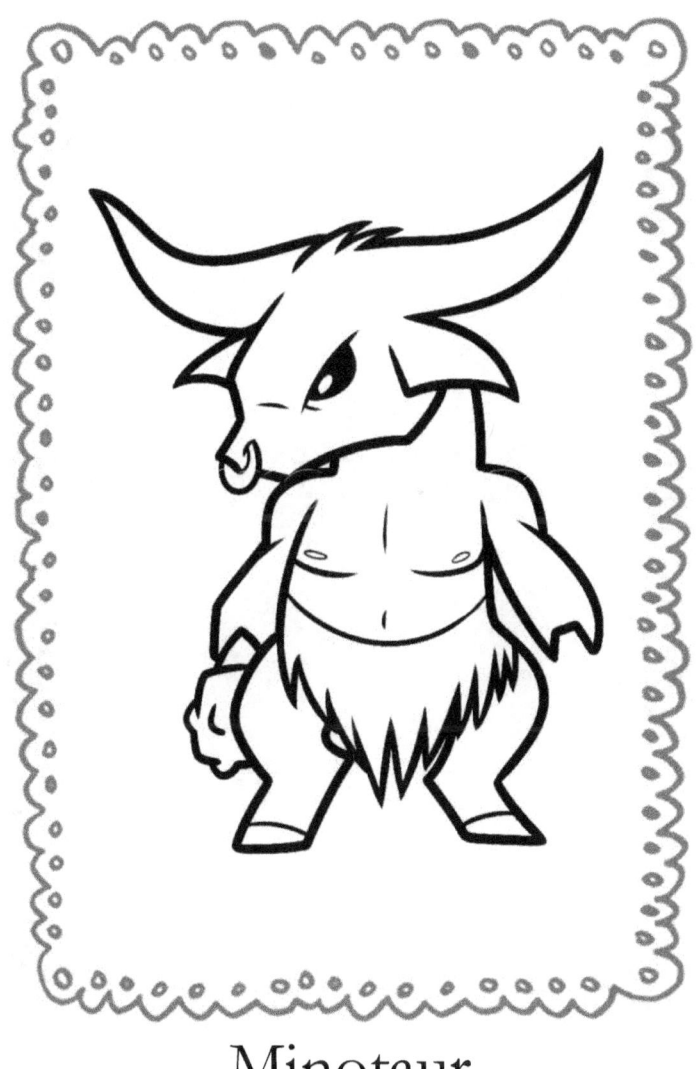

Minotaur

STEP 1.

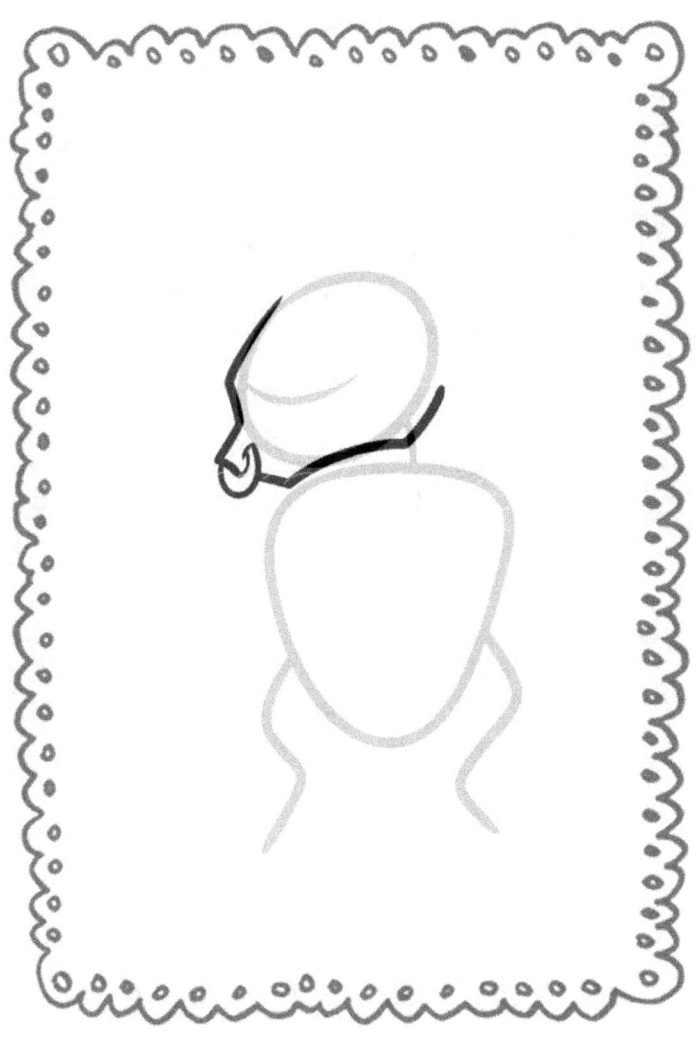

STEP 2.

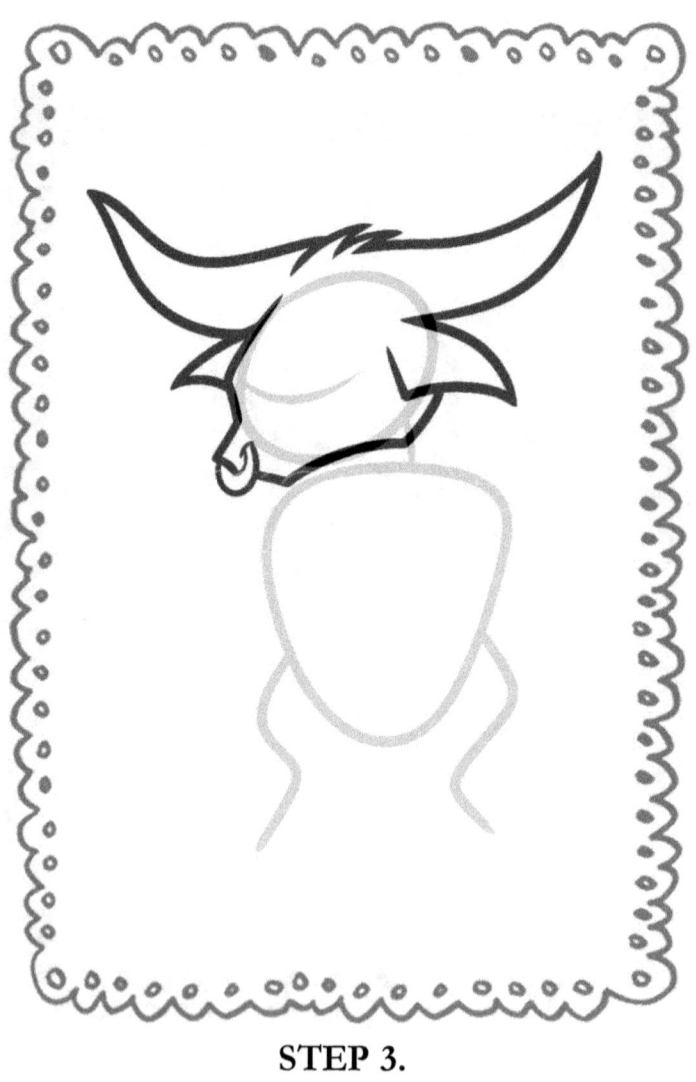

STEP 3.

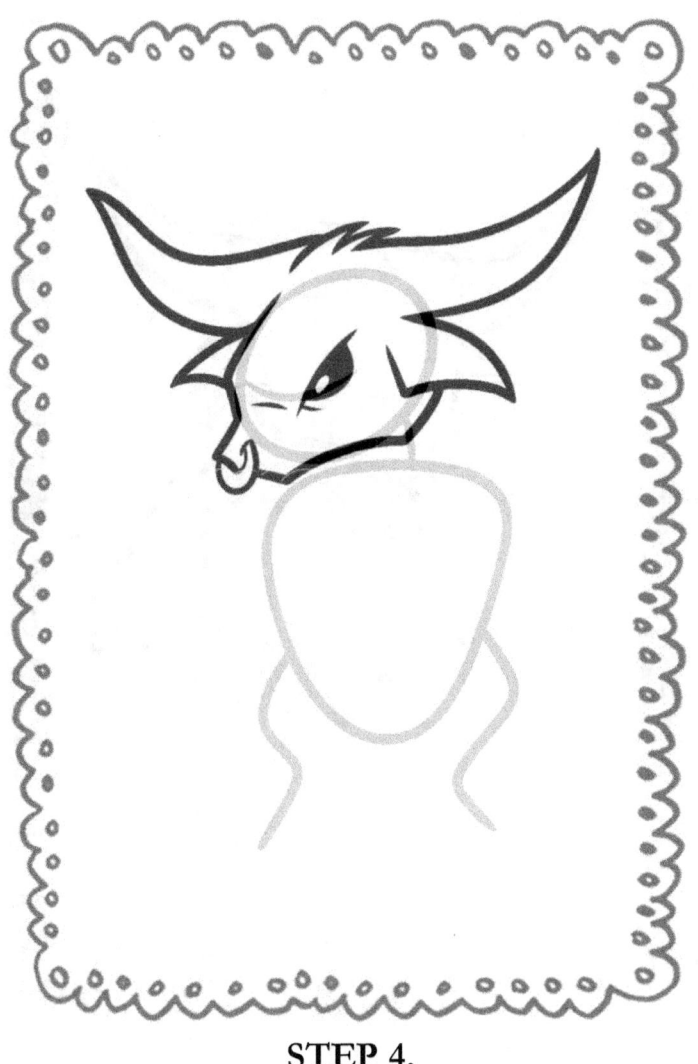

STEP 4.

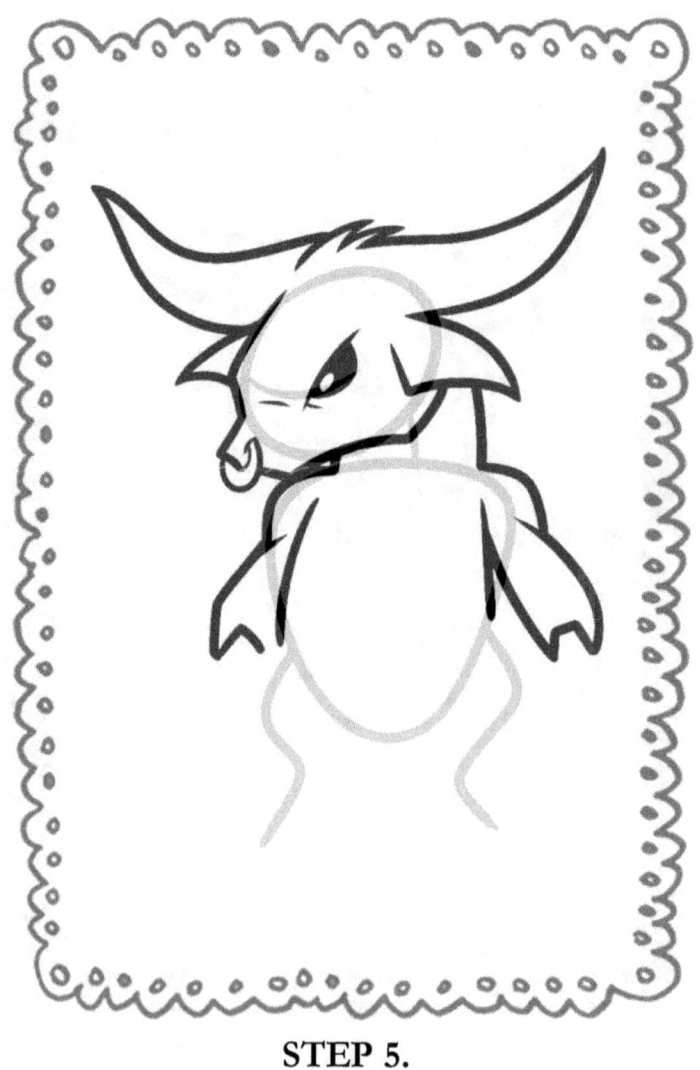

STEP 5.

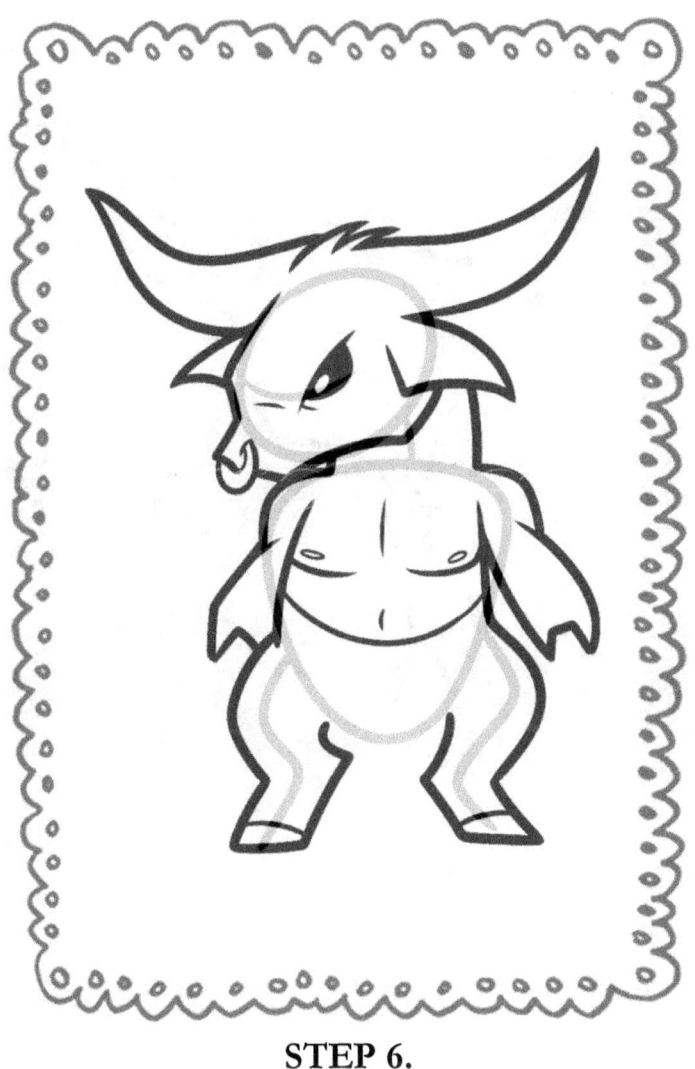

STEP 6.

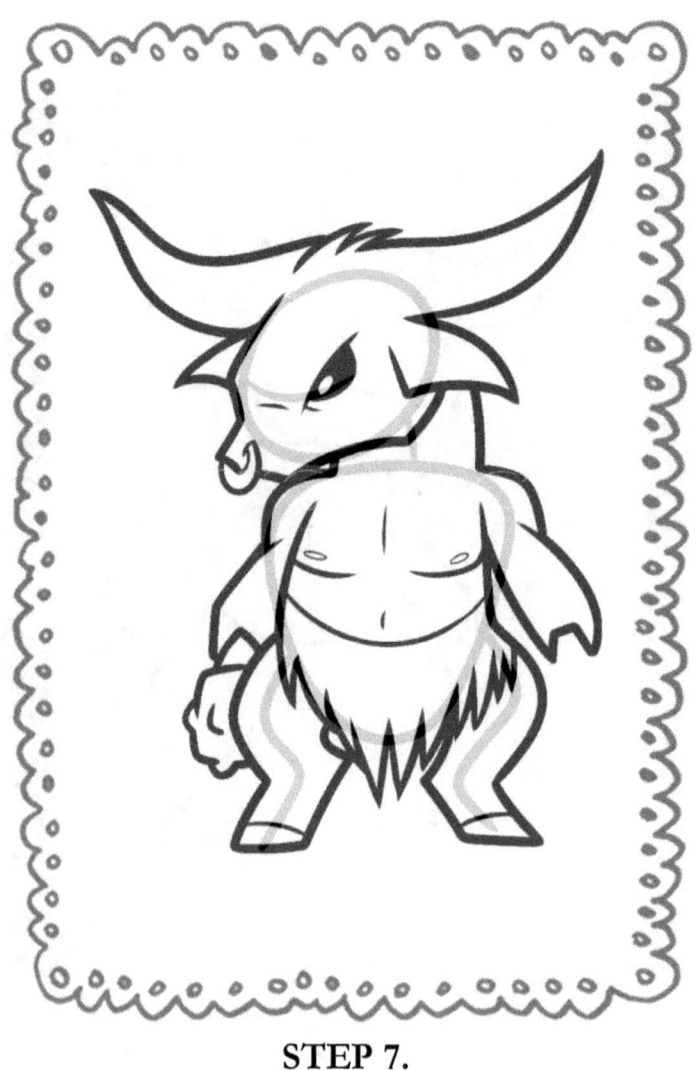

STEP 7.

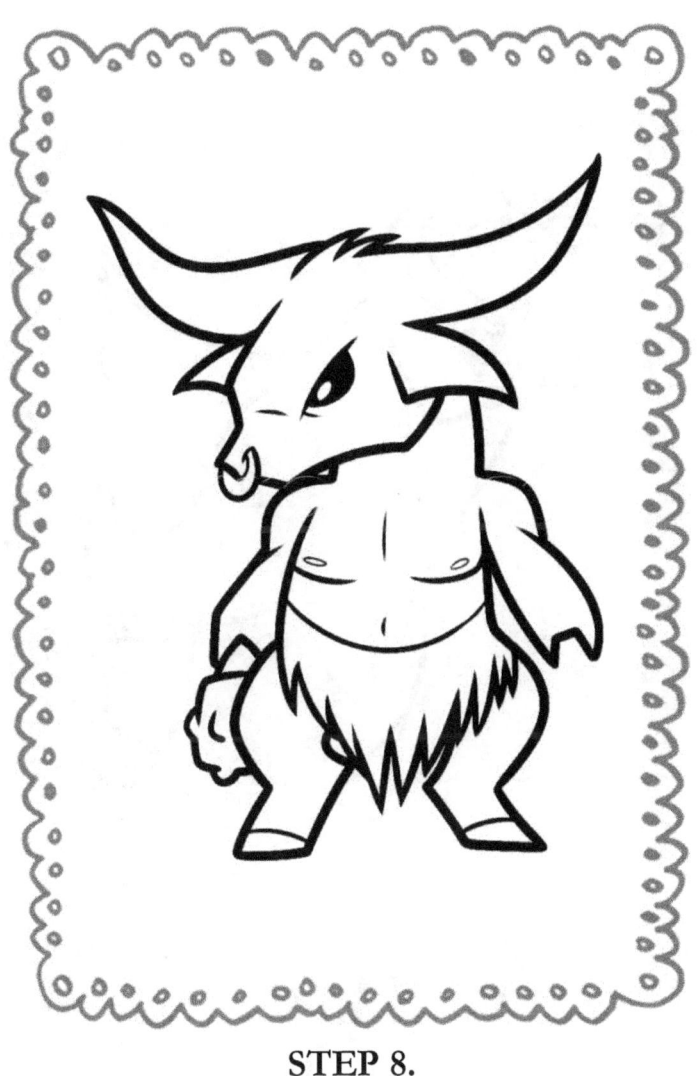

STEP 8.

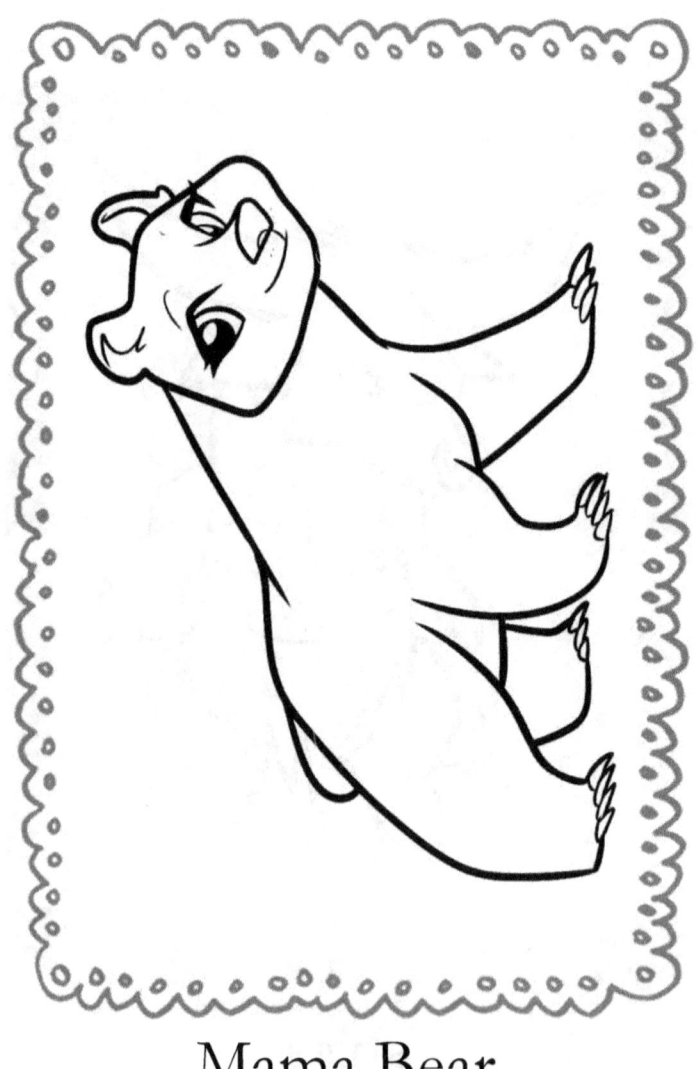

Mama Bear

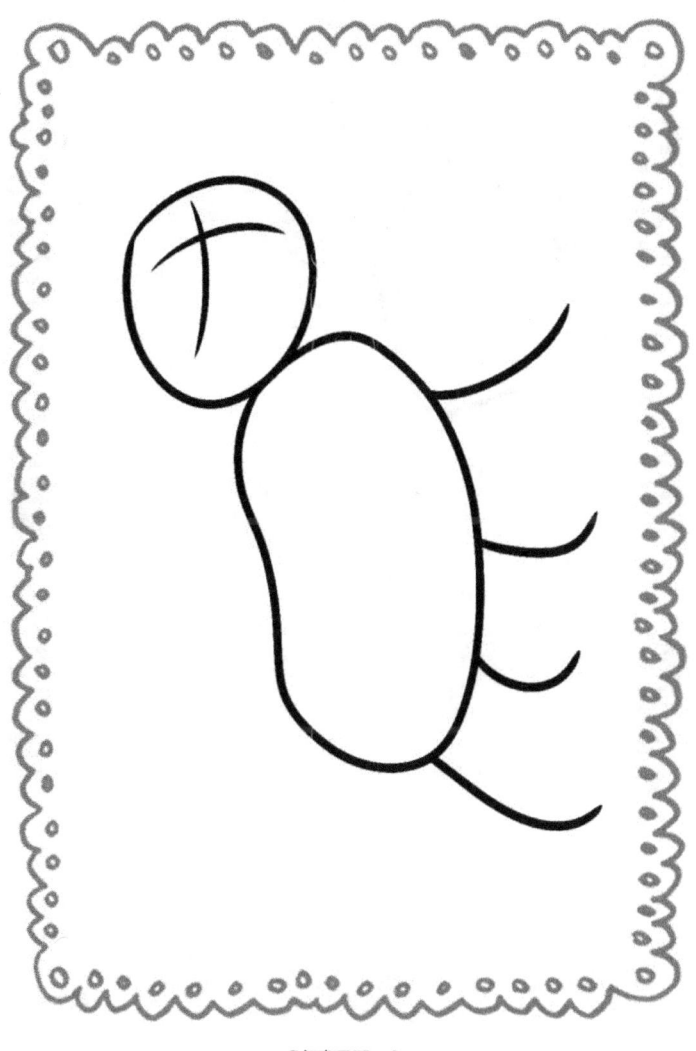

STEP 1.

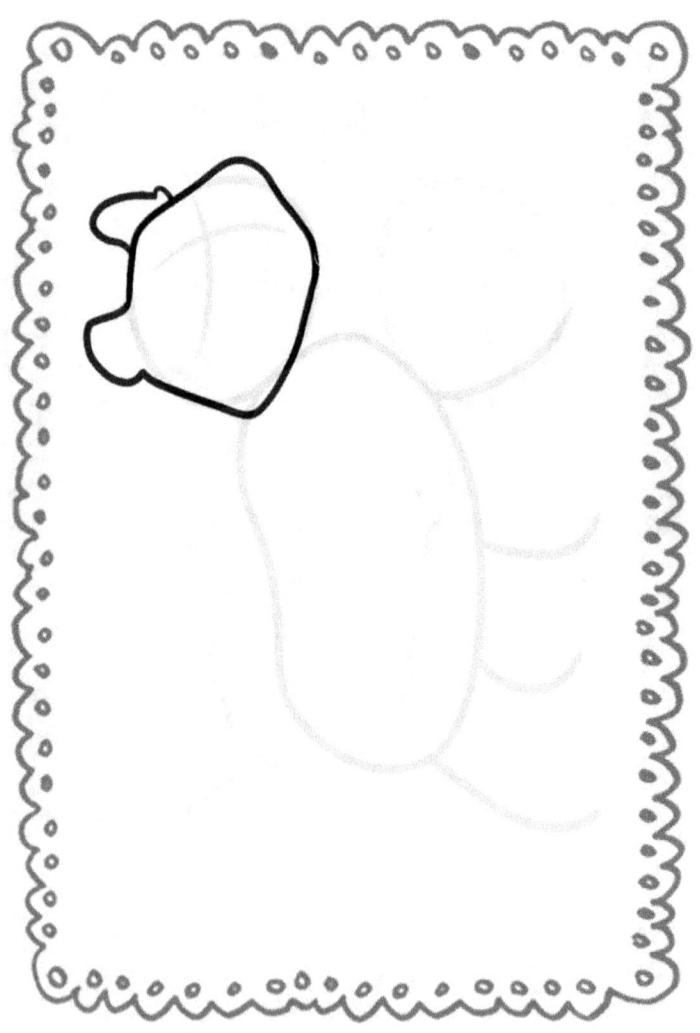

STEP 2.

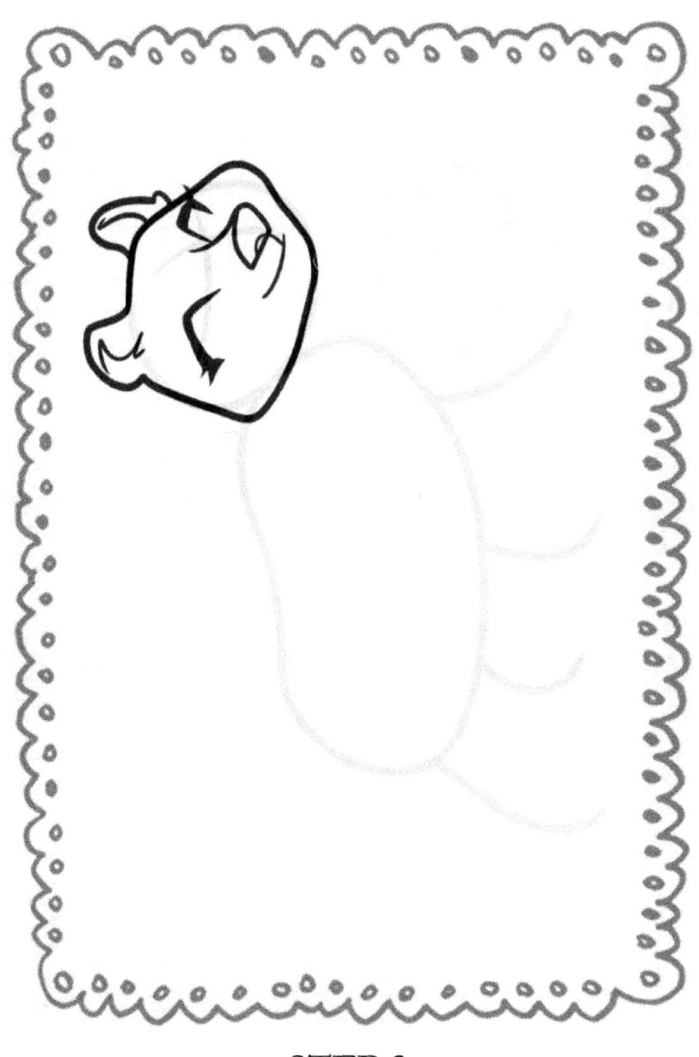

STEP 3.

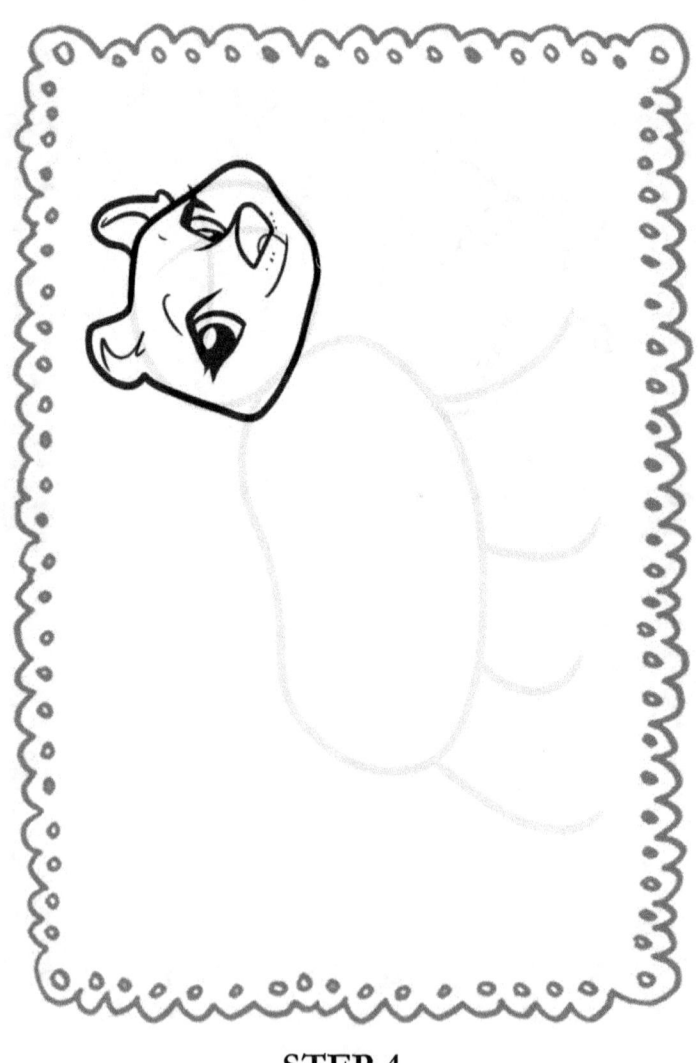

STEP 4.

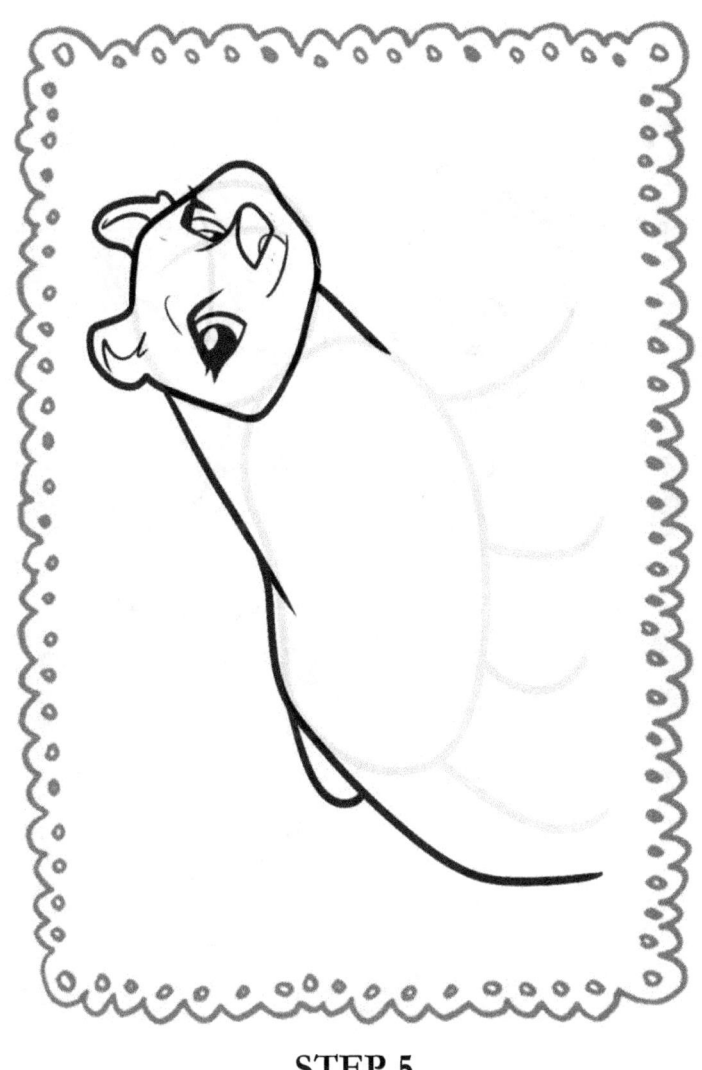

STEP 5.

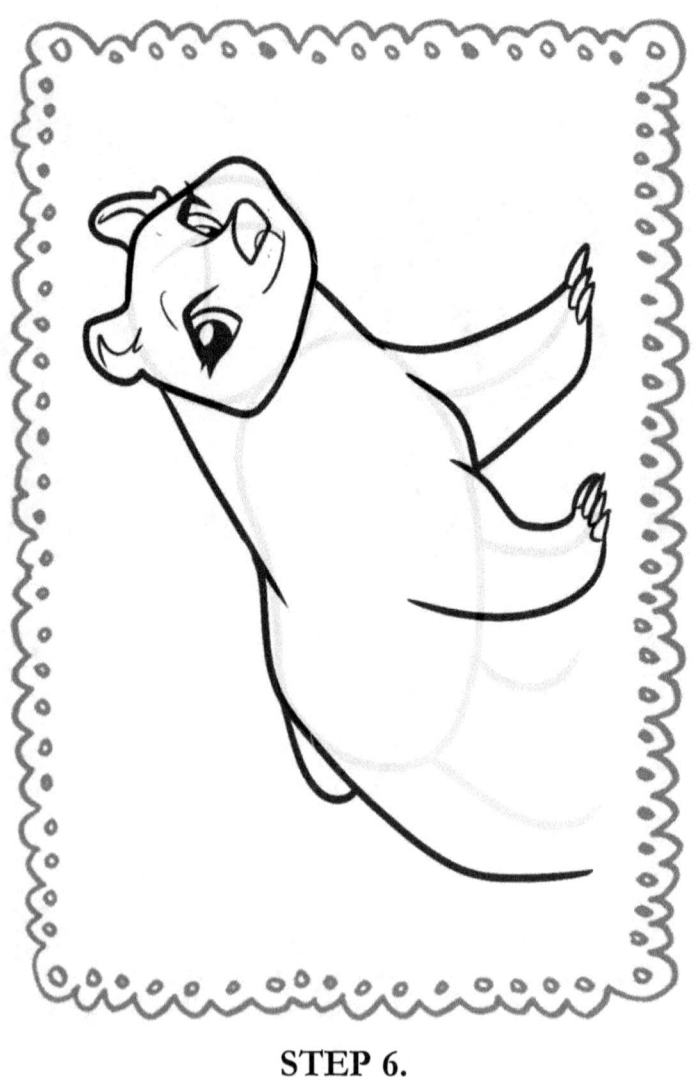

STEP 6.

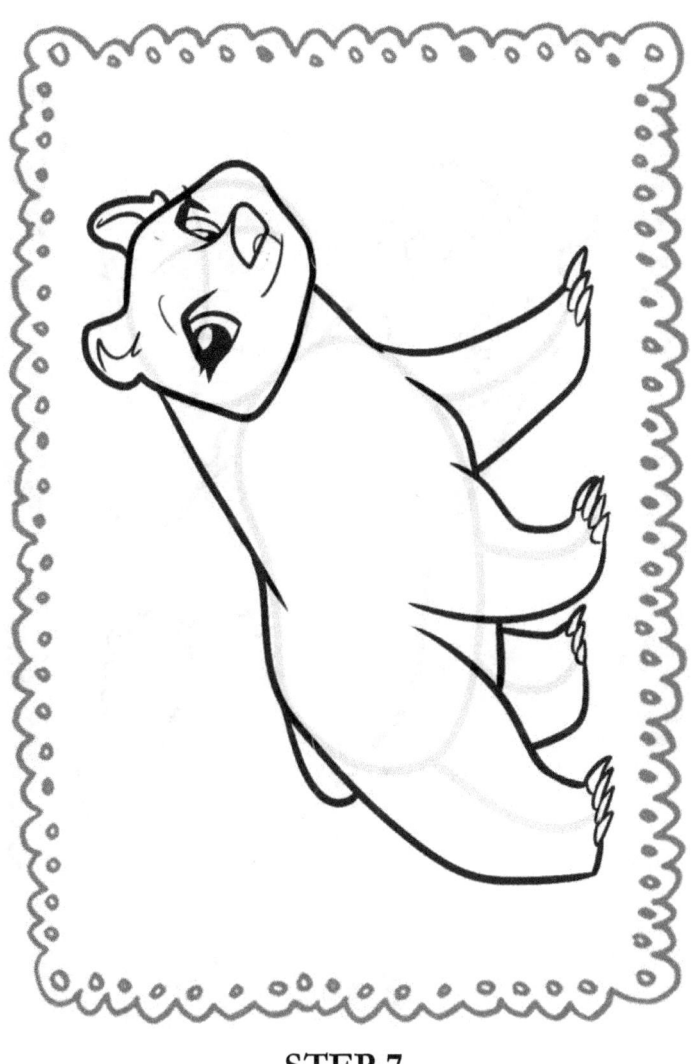

STEP 7.

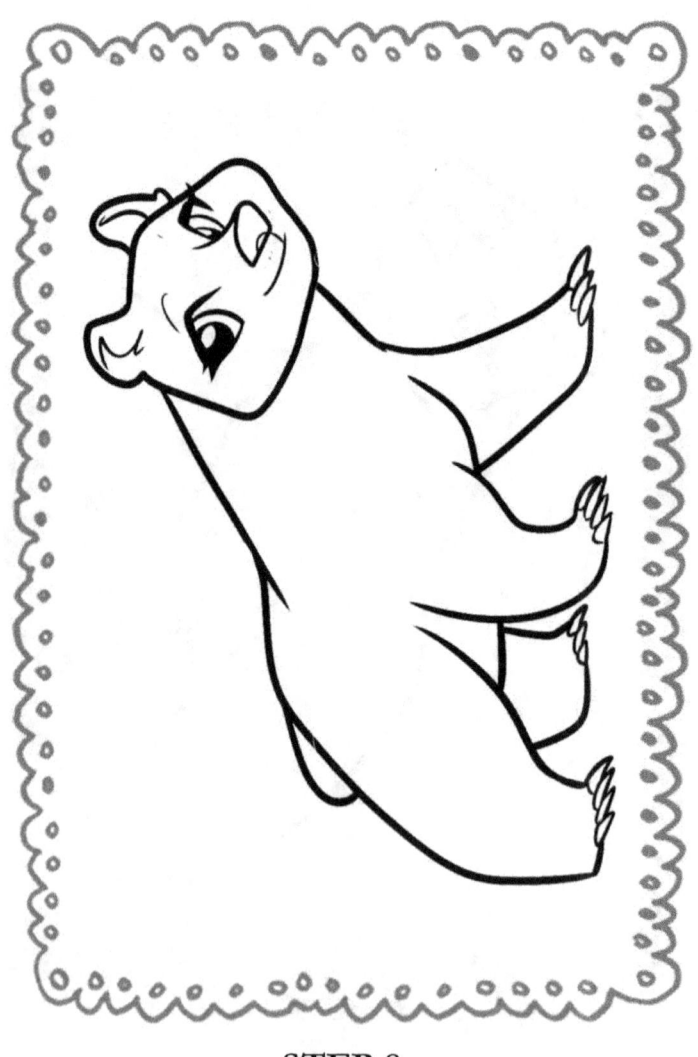

STEP 8.

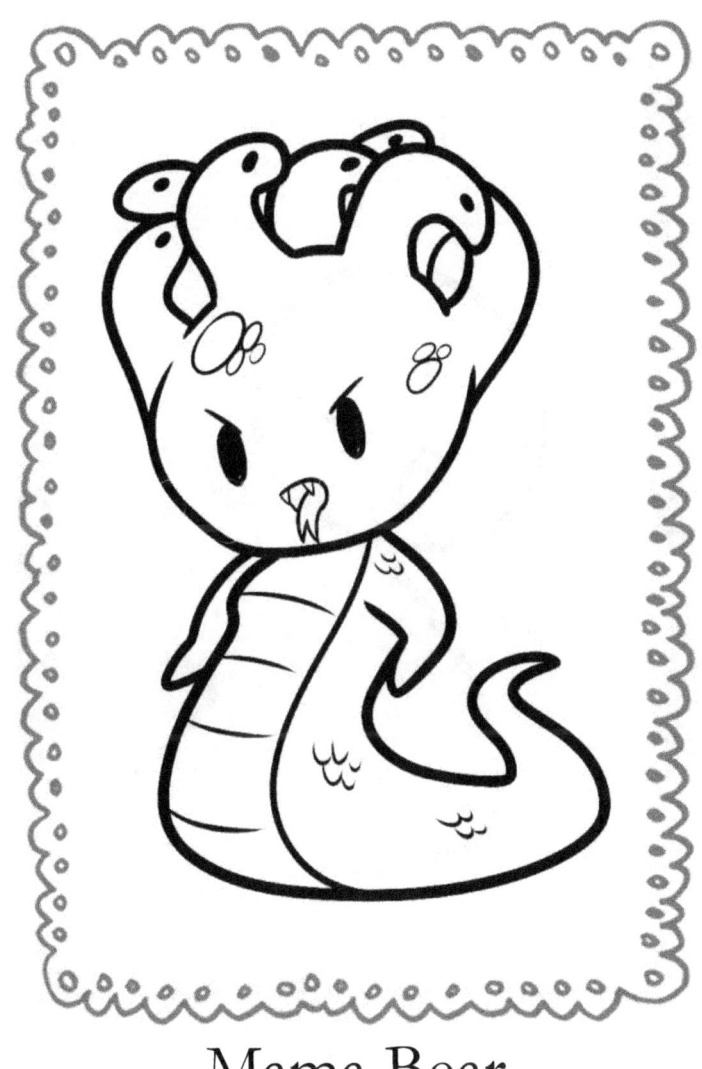

Mama Bear

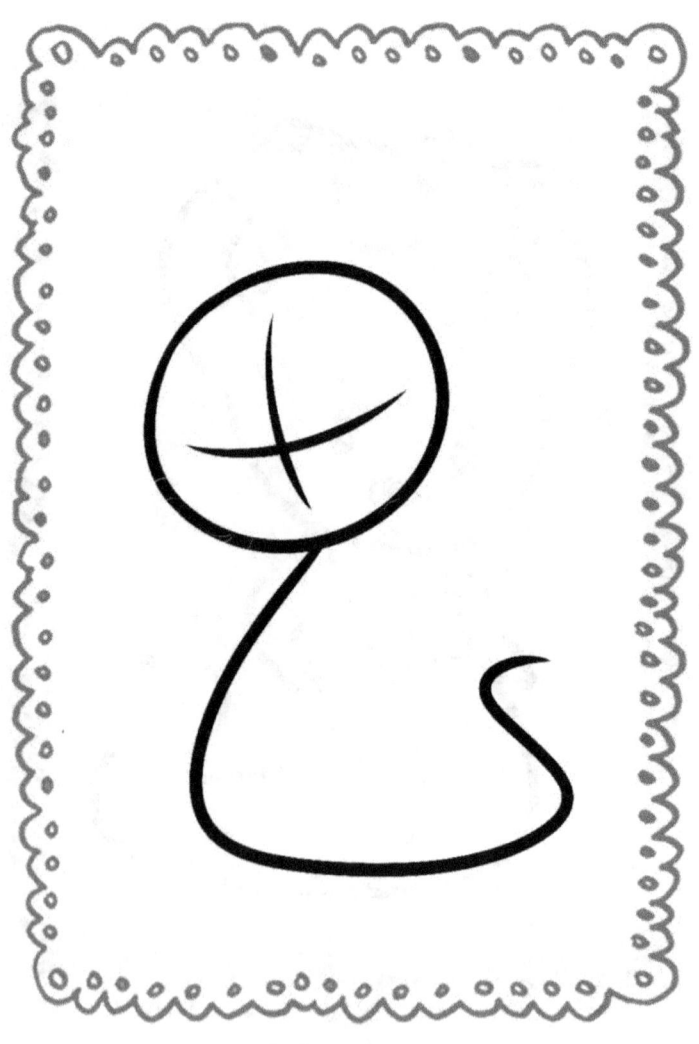

STEP 1.

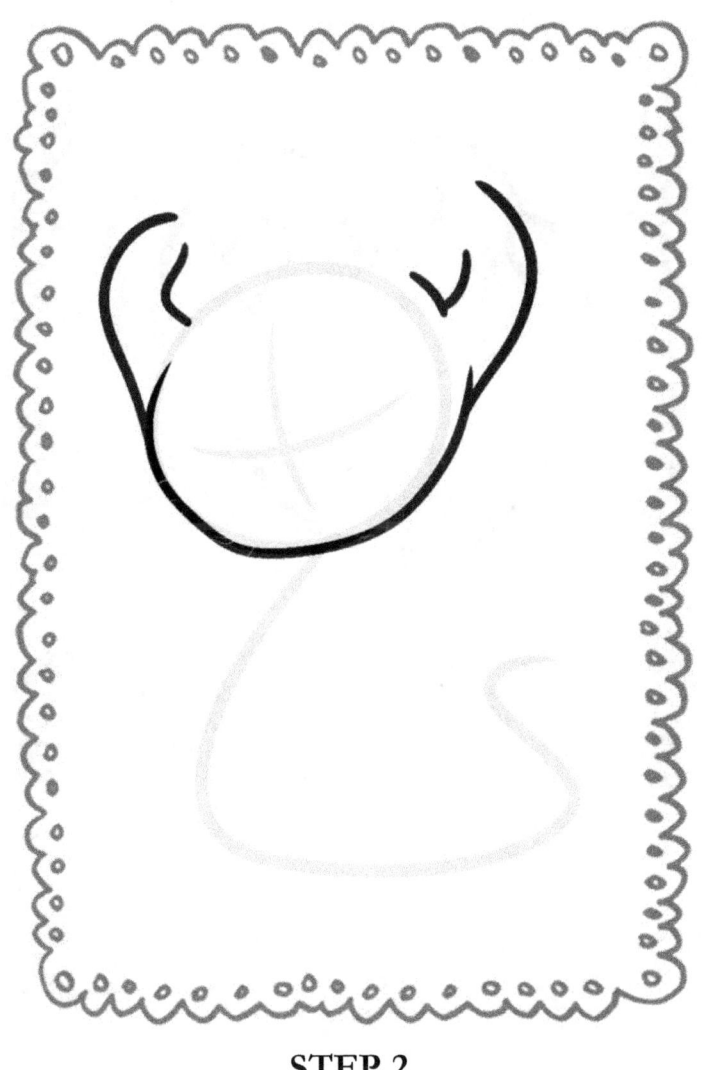

STEP 2.

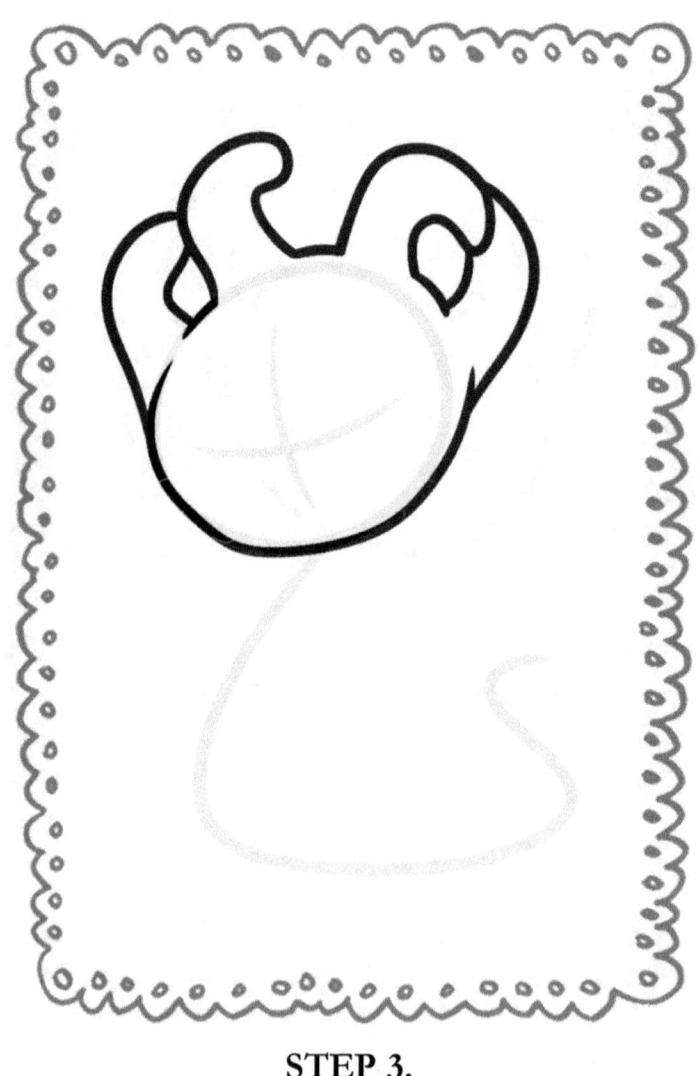

STEP 3.

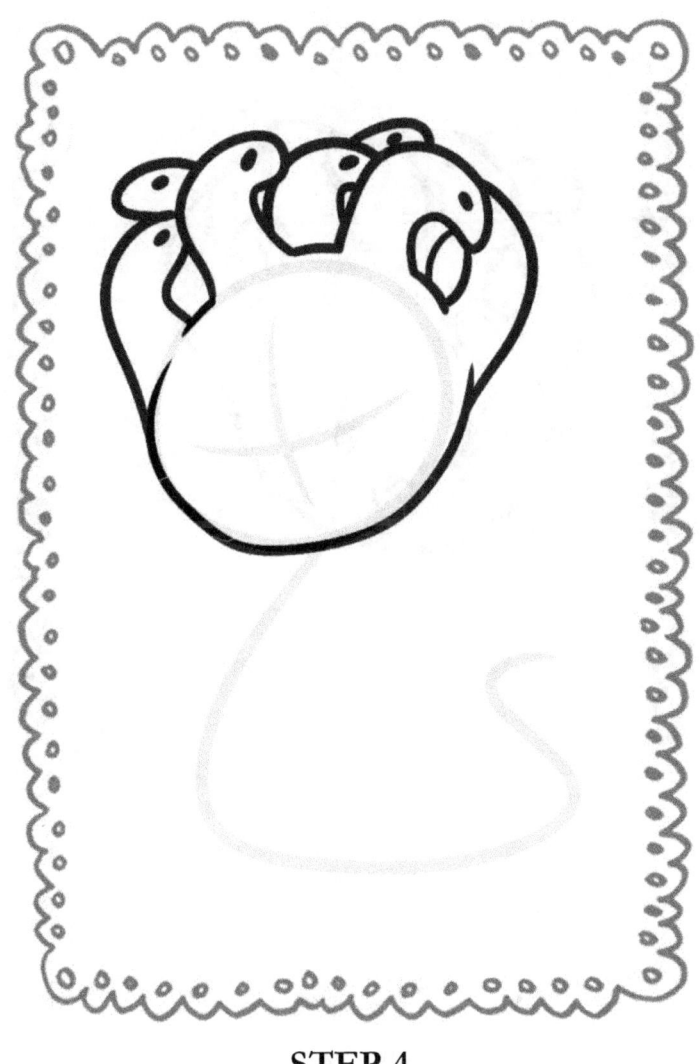

STEP 4.

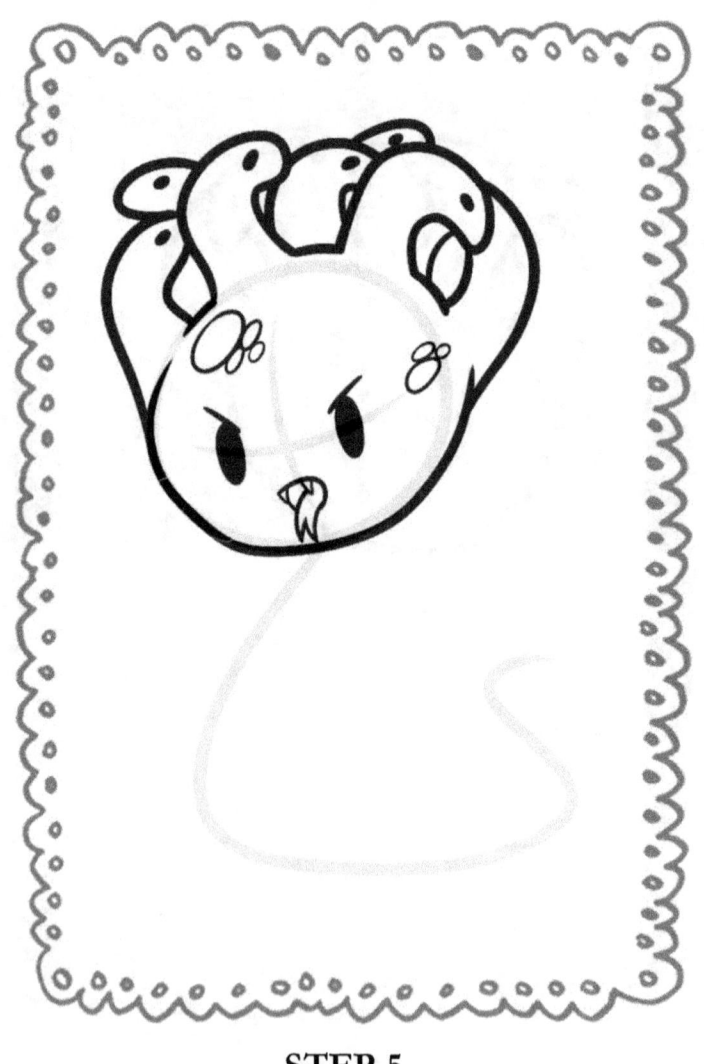

STEP 5.

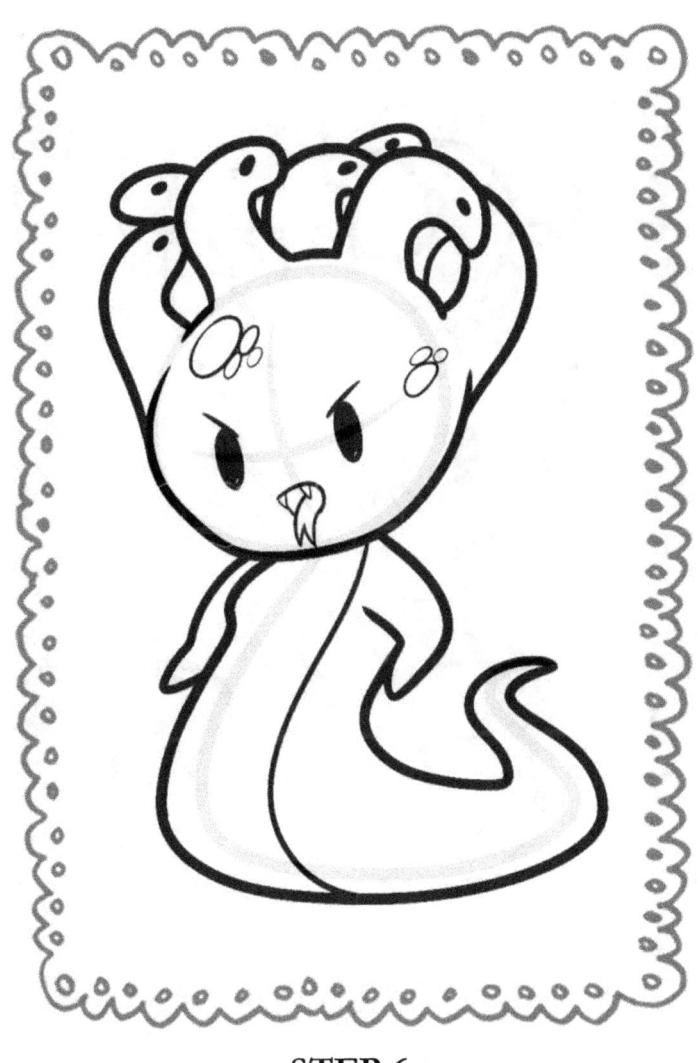

STEP 6.

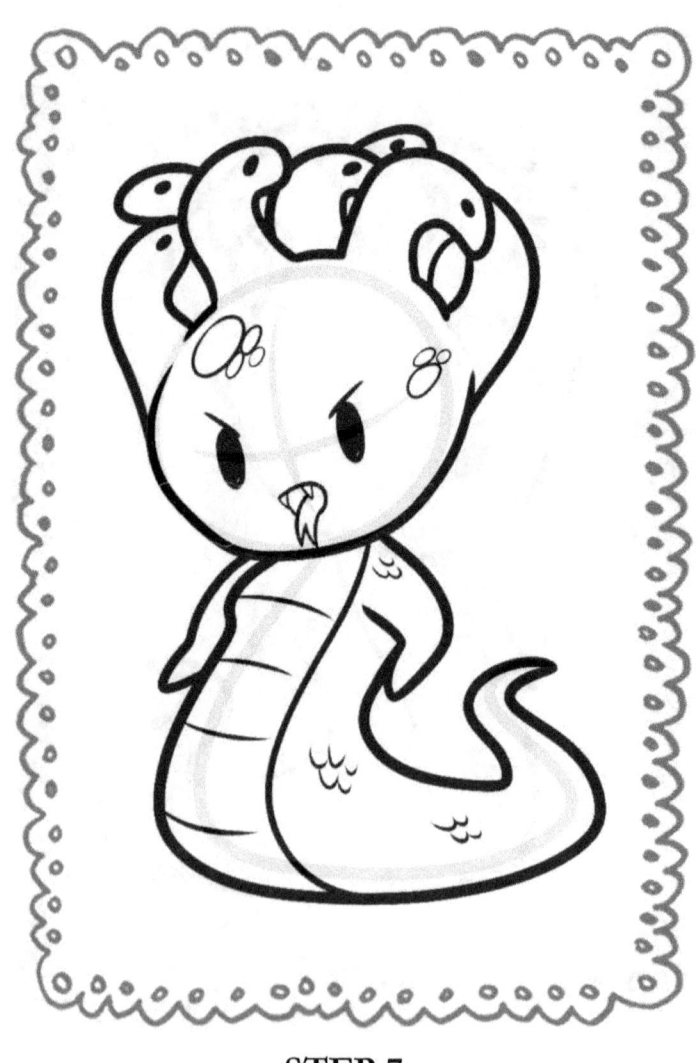

STEP 7.

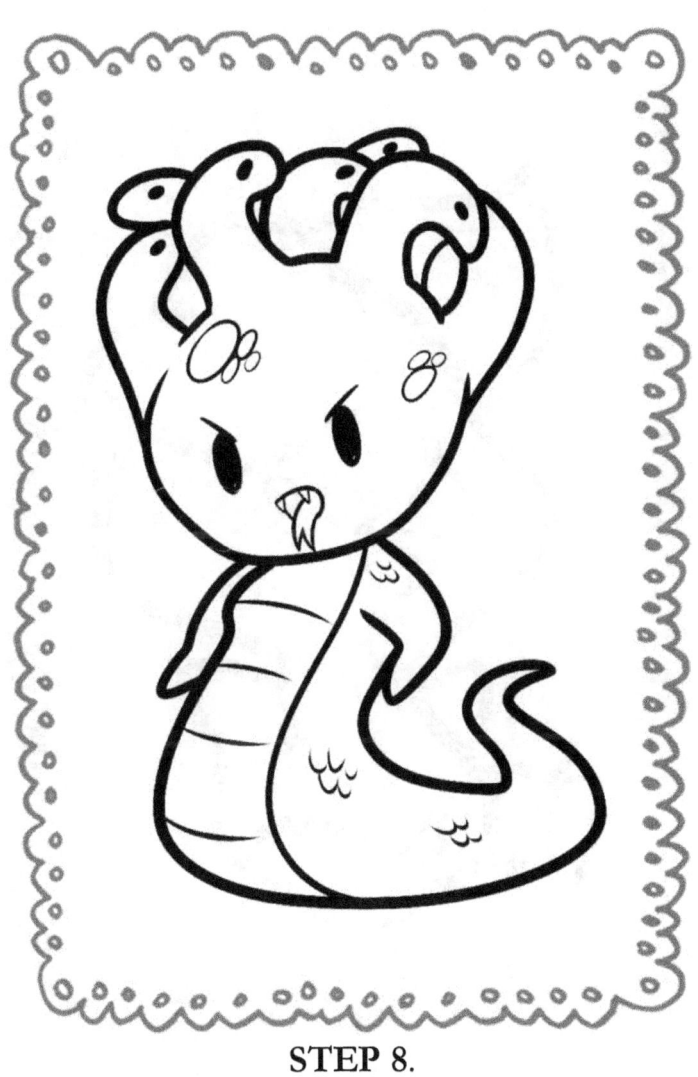

STEP 8.

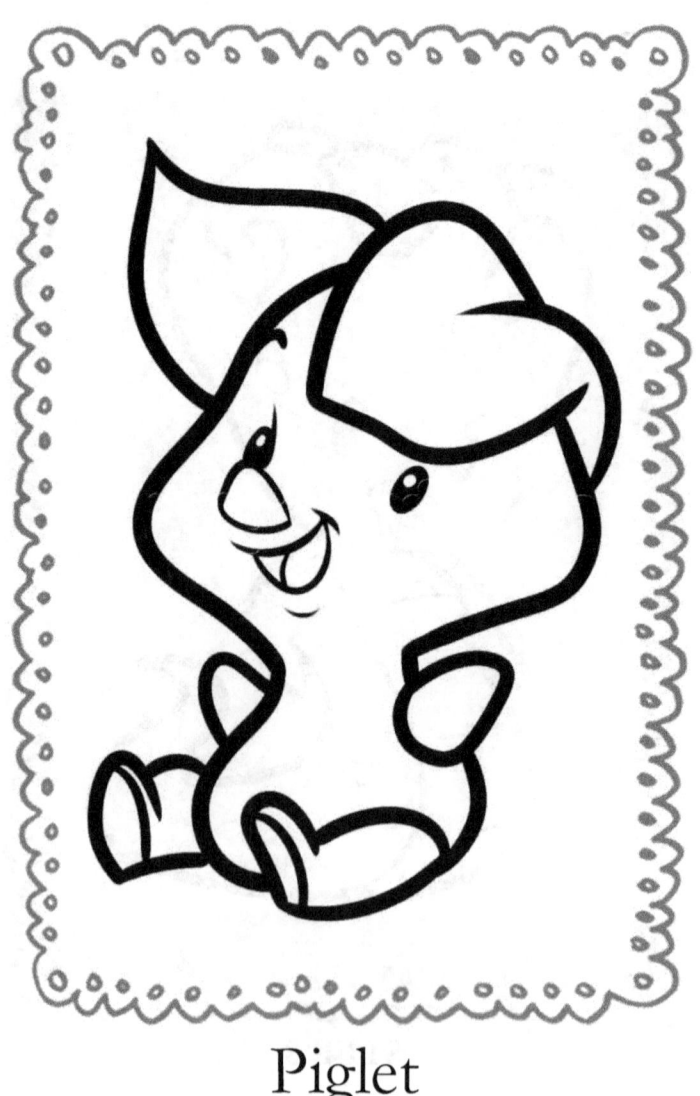

Piglet

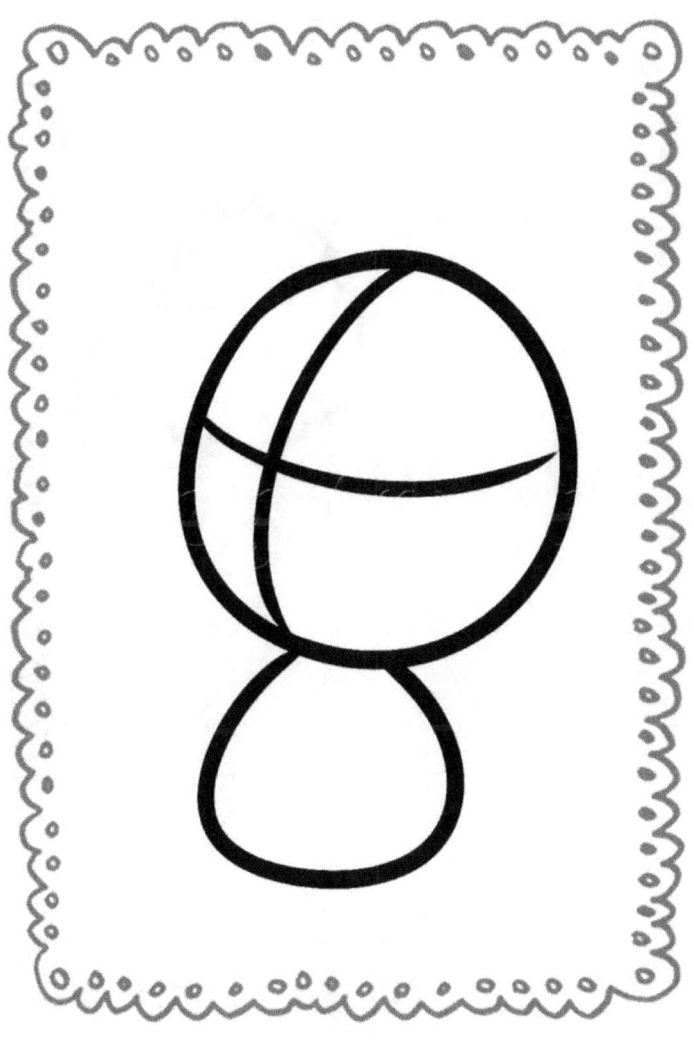

STEP 1.

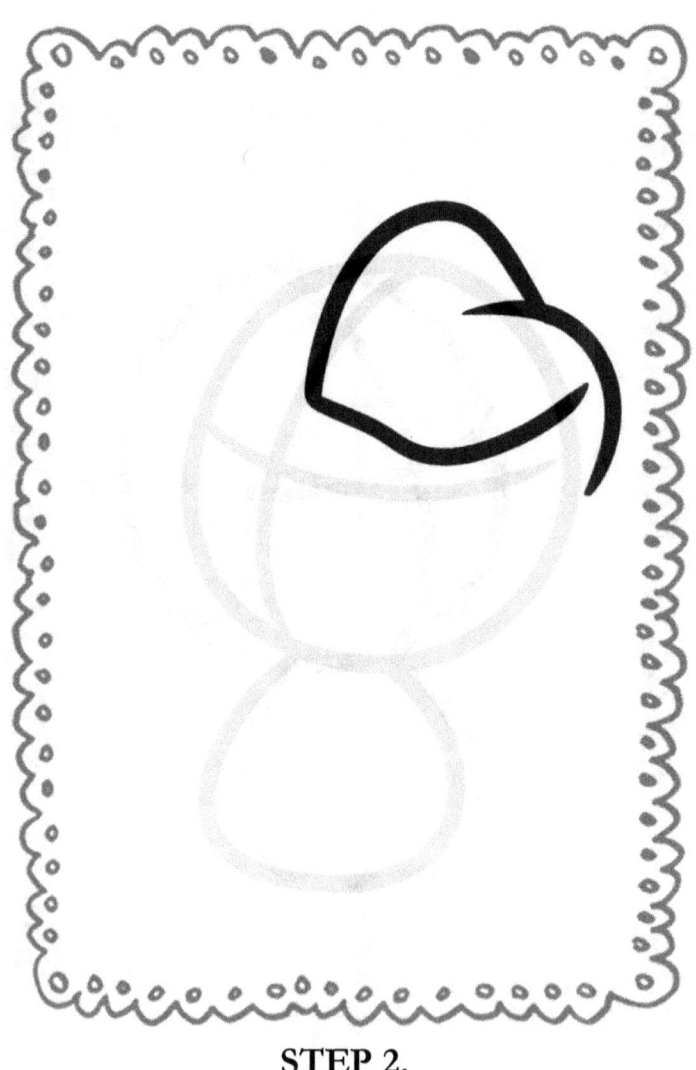

STEP 2.

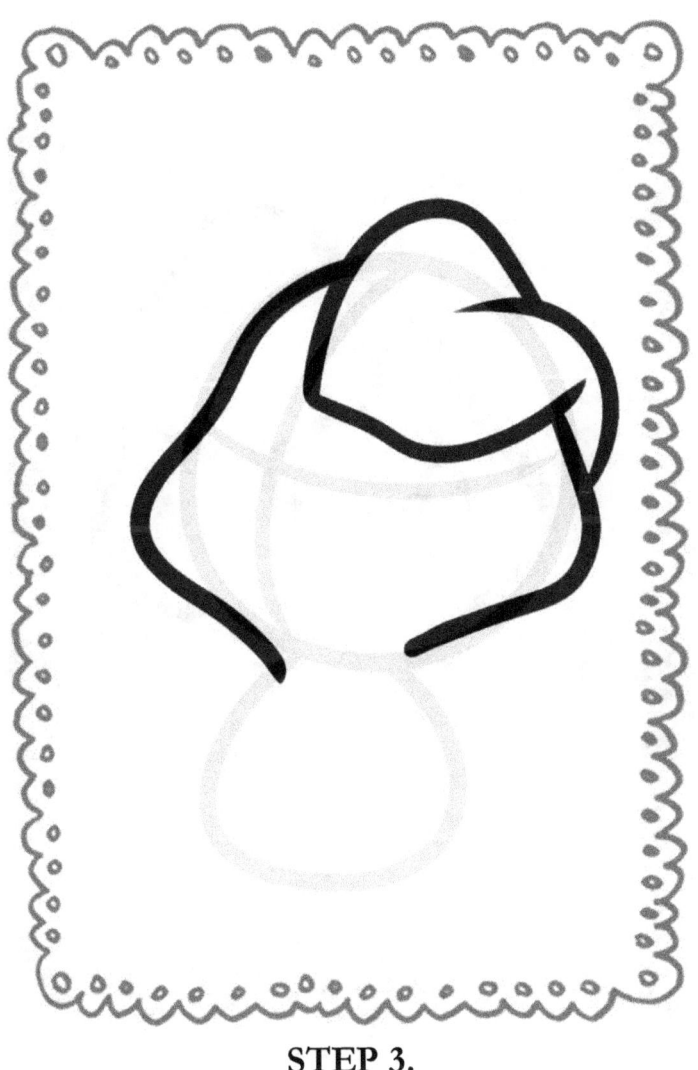

STEP 3.

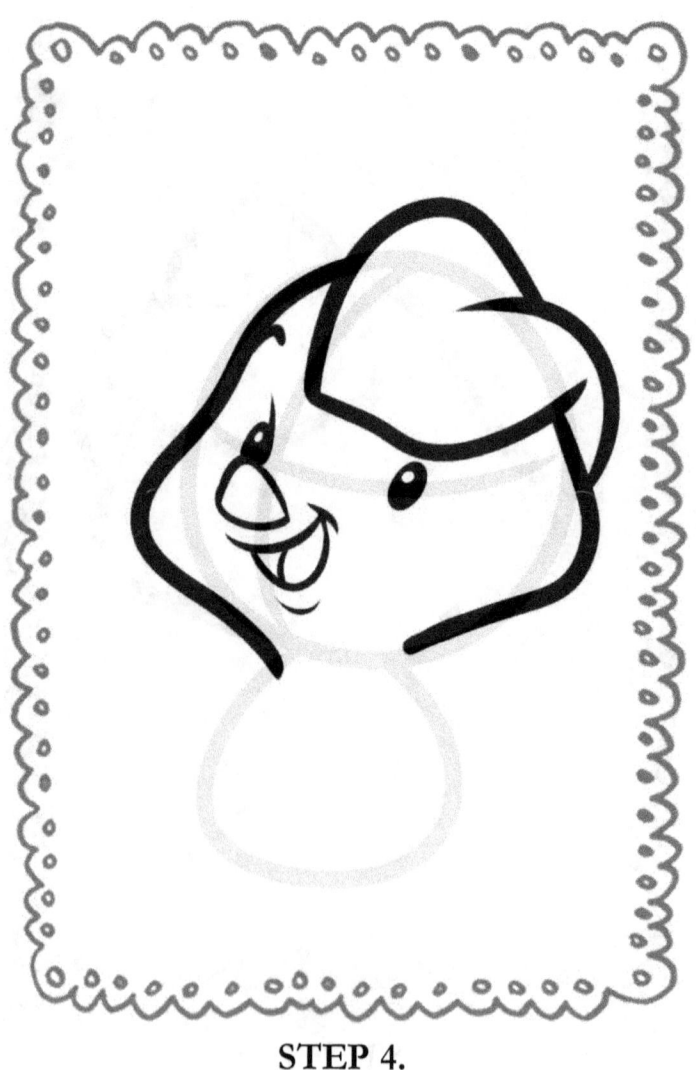

STEP 4.

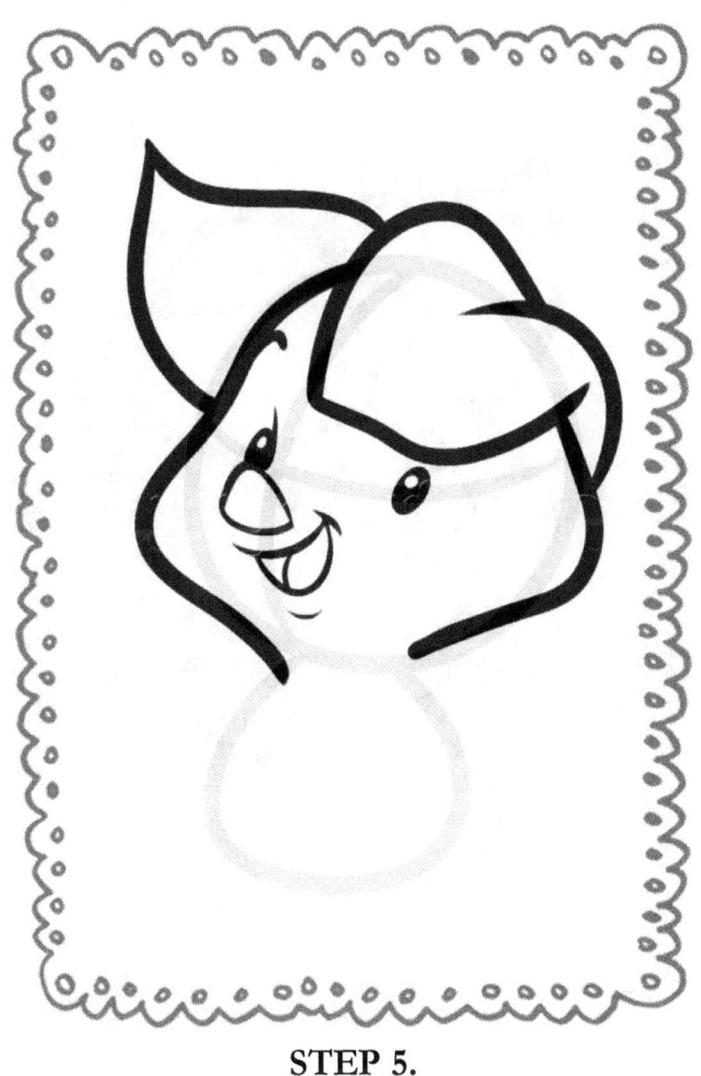

STEP 5.

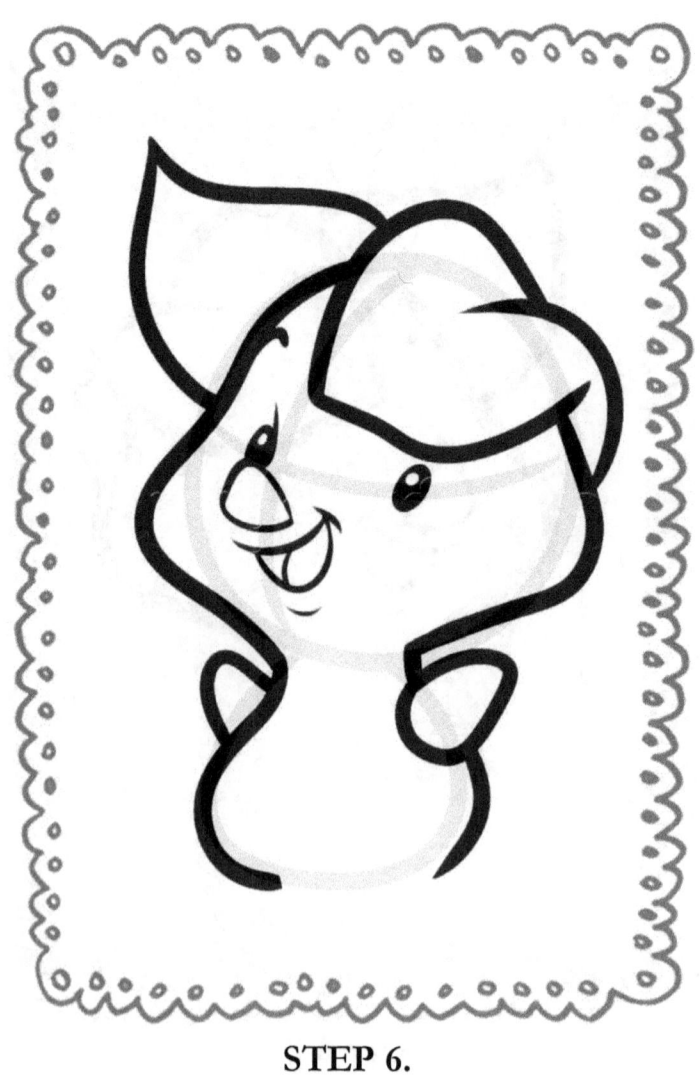

STEP 6.

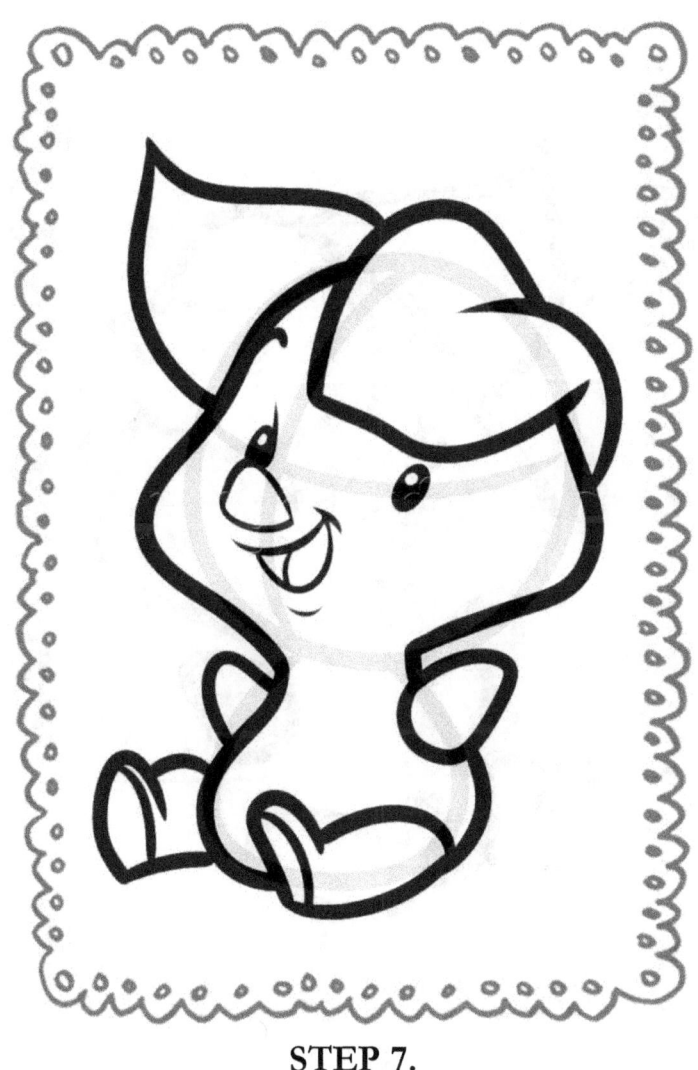

STEP 7.

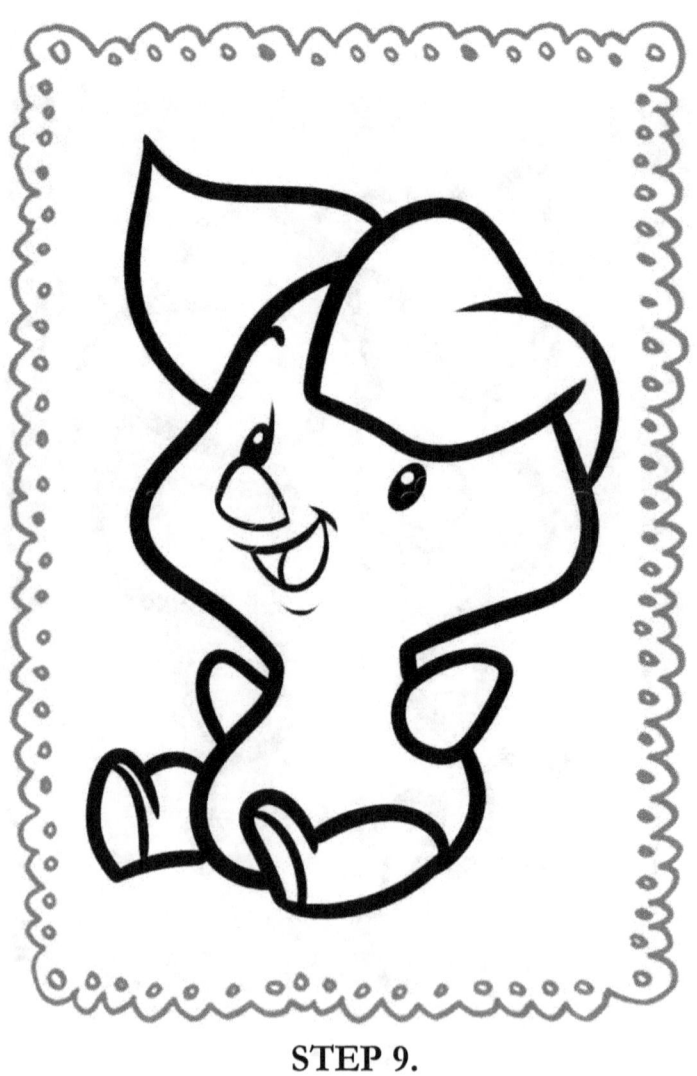

STEP 9.